The Centre of Attraction at

THE MOTOR CYCLE,
8 NOVEMBER 1951

STAND Nº

MODEL G80S
498 c.c. O.H.V.

MATCHLESS
Clubman

ZHANG SEN
1942–

An elegant balance

112 Zhang Sen's work graces more than a dozen of China's major cultural sites. Here he is shown, in 1988, in front of his inscription by the beautiful Slender West Lake at Yangzhou in Jiangsu province.

Zhang Sen is one of the leading practitioners of Neo-Classical calligraphy. Several reviewers have said that his simple, elegant style has opened up a new path in the development of the art. One went so far as to add that his work was not only a source of great pleasure, but also 'a model that would benefit our culture'. The attractiveness of his work – with its elegant rhythms and balances – and the appeal of its content have made Zhang Sen's pieces very popular. They have also made him one of the most highly paid calligraphers in China.

His success is due first and foremost to the quality of his art. However, his extrovert personality and rugged individualism help to widen his circle of admirers still further. An exceptionally active man, he is frequently to be found swimming in icy pools in winter, racing from meeting to meeting on a motorbike (more recently, in a car), endlessly communicating with people on his mobile phone, or delighting in Western classical music played at high volume on his world-class sound system.

One of the few

Zhang Sen began his studies in calligraphy before the Cultural Revolution. His achievements can be seen as all the greater for the fact that he had no privileged introduction into the art. At the age of four he received his first lessons in calligraphy from his father, a middle-school teacher serving with the Communists' New Fourth Army, which at that time was based in Zhejiang province.

In the early 1950s the family moved to Shanghai. Although Zhang Sen had a good technical education, he was given little encouragement to develop his calligraphy. At school he showed that he was gifted with numbers (if you tell him your date of birth he can quickly calculate which day of the week it was) and good at solving practical problems. Had there not been five children in the family, he would no doubt have gone on to university. Instead, after graduating from high school he went to work in a factory as a technician, where he specialized in optics. As time went by he began designing optical equipment, for which he won a number of awards.

Whilst employed as a technician, Zhang Sen pursued calligraphy as a hobby. Traditionally, Chinese calligraphers devote years to disciplined practice before becoming masters of the art. But few of the younger ones have had the time or inclination to follow this path, preferring the easier route of developing styles that are not dependent on such experience. In this respect, Zhang Sen is a rare exception. His flair for calligraphy and his determination to practise it attracted the interest of a number of Shanghai's best calligraphers, who by then were all quite advanced in years: in particular, Pan Xuegu, Weng Kaiyun, Wang Juchang and Ren Zhen. From them he learned that, even without being a scholar of Chinese culture, he would be able to create fine calligraphy if he gained mastery of classical techniques before cultivating his own style and sensibility.

The Cultural Revolution had less effect on Zhang Sen's life than on that of many other calligraphers featured in this book. In 1966 he was still working at the factory in Shanghai; two years later, at the age of twenty-six, he was made deputy chief of its technical branch. The factory was engaged in designing instruments for manufacture within China, to avoid such equipment having to be imported. Those who had most influence over the events in Shanghai therefore had no wish to see its operations thrown into chaos. So, even during the Cultural Revolution, Zhang Sen enjoyed a certain degree of 'job security'. In his spare time he continued to study and practise calligraphy.

By the beginning of the 1970s the situation in Shanghai was sufficiently calm for him to see his former teachers again. To his delight, he was also able to visit the elderly Shen Yinmo (by now an almost legendary figure in the world of Chinese calligraphy) just before his death in 1971. While continuing to work at the factory, Zhang Sen devoted most of his free time to improving his calligraphy. In particular, he took a keen interest in the firm-lined and beautifully balanced clerical script of the Han dynasty (206 BC–AD 220).

Two years later one of Zhang Sen's pieces was included in the first calligraphy exhibition to be held in Shanghai since the start of the Cultural Revolution. His work was rated so highly that he was invited to join the Shanghai Calligraphy and Seal-Carving Association, at that time one of only two such bodies in China. Through the Association, in 1977 Zhang Sen met Lin Sanzhi (pp. 140–5), who five years earlier had become China's most admired contemporary calligrapher virtually overnight.

In 1980, after Deng Xiaoping had set China on the road to economic reform and begun to revitalize the arts, Zhang Sen was finally able to turn professional as a calligrapher by joining the staff of the Chinese Painting Institute of Shanghai. There he devoted much of his time to studying the history of calligraphy and developing his technical skill, particularly in

writing clerical and running scripts. In 1985 he co-authored a textbook on calligraphy for university students. In the same year, he and his friend Professor Liu Zengfu (pp. 203–9) published their book *A Basic Knowledge of Clerical Script*, which has since sold some 150,000 copies. In his influential essay *The Analysis of Brush Technique* (1986) Zhang Sen examined what earlier masters had said on this subject, as well as putting forward his own advice on the points he deemed most relevant to contemporary calligraphers. He so impressed the leaders of the Institute with these publications, and with his own calligraphy, that in 1988, at the age of forty-six, he was appointed a professor.

Creating art

It is generally accepted that a calligrapher's distinctive style does not fully emerge until late in his life. However, even in his early thirties Zhang Sen had begun to think that unless he soon adopted a style of his own, he would never be able to create 'art'.

In the clerical and running scripts for which he has become best known, he started then to devise his rich amalgamation of the elements of earlier styles, in which his brushwork is executed with exemplary skill. Although this work is innovative in style and fresh in appearance, Zhang Sen has ensured that in both these scripts his calligraphy remains squarely within the mainstream of the Grand Tradition. He does this, he says, because it is what the vast majority of people like. This is why he produces calligraphy that induces calm, rather than seeking the excitement and tension that has a greater appeal among intellectuals.

A popular text that Zhang Sen chose for one of his works was the poem *Ferrying South to Lizhou* (fig. 113) by Wen Tingyun (813–870). For the Chinese, the name Fan Li, which occurs at the end of the poem, conjures up a spicy mixture of images: sound judgement, women, money, contentment. During the Warring States period (475–221 BC), when Wu and Yue were at war, Fan Li advised the King of Yue to send beautiful women to the King of Wu in order to sap his strength. The success of Fan Li's recommendation led the King of Yue to offer him the post of prime minister. Fan Li declined the honour, asking instead for permission to become a merchant. His wish was granted. He subsequently made a vast amount of money, and lived to enjoy it by the misty waters of the Five Lakes, reputedly in company with the most beautiful of the women who had been sent to the King of Wu.

Zhang Sen shuns the ongoing debate over whether calligraphy is valid only when traditional in style, as he feels that different styles should be allowed to coexist. Nevertheless, he is a staunch champion of quality and

Detail of fig. 114

113 These four panels of Zhang Sen's calligraphy contain the classical poem *Ferrying South to Lizhou*. It is a well-known text evoking a mood of calm:

Placidly, the bare waters face the sunset.
Jagged islets blend a sober green with
*   mountain mists.*
A horse neighs over the ripples –
*   as I watch, the boatmen pole away.*

Men rest beside the willows,
*   waiting for the ferry's return.*
A flock of gulls veers over the dune grass.
And above the acres of river meadows,
*   a single egret wings its way.*

Has anyone the wisdom to embark
*   and search for Fan Li,*
Who, alone, learned to forget on the
*   misty waters of the Five Lakes?*

198

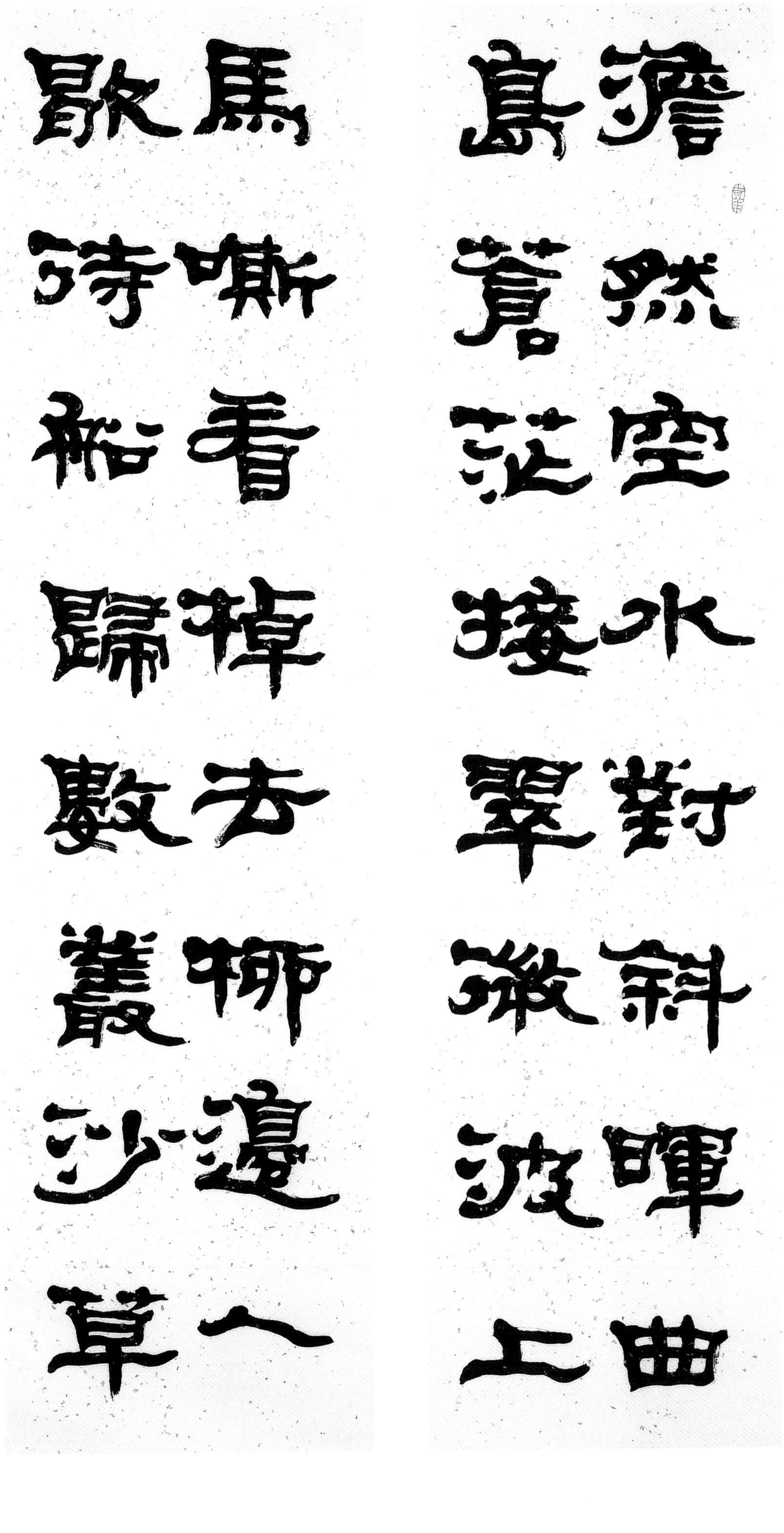

灣然空水對斜暉曲
島蒼茫接翠微波上
馬嘶看掉去柳邊人
歌詩秥歸數叢沙草

integrity. The best results, he argues, are achieved by observing the well-established convention of exploiting the tip of the brush, not 'slashing about' with the sides of it. He insists that calligraphy is about art, which cannot be attained purely through technique. In his opinion, writing out a couple of Chinese characters with gusto does not constitute the art of calligraphy. If calligraphy is to merit being described as art, it must have magic in the words rather than just being a display of mastery of the brush.

Recognizing that the clock cannot be turned back, Zhang Sen says it is likely that within a few years no one in China will be able to compose a classical Chinese poem. Even now, there are few people left who can write classical Chinese prose. This means that the content of works of calligraphy will have to be taken either from quotations from the masters of the past or from modern Chinese texts that purport to have some kind of classical flavour. This prospect does not depress him, though. He feels that, through excellence of technique and a judicious selection of texts that appeal to the present generation, great pleasure and meaning can still be conveyed.

Zhang Sen is renowned for the clear, smooth, lively lines of his running script. These qualities fit perfectly with the delightful poem *The Evening of the Lantern Festival* by Xin Qiji (1140–1207), which he chose as the content of a work he produced in 1994 (fig. 114). The verses conjure up the delights of life under the Southern Song dynasty and highlight men's enduring fascination with beguiling women:

Into an easterly wind, fireworks burst out,
   like a thousand trees and flowers,
   then come down like falling stars.

The fragrance from bejewelled carriages fills the avenue,
   while, throughout the night, tunes flow from flutes
   and fish- and dragon-dancers prance.

Women with hair cascading like golden willow tresses,
   laugh and chat, then vanish in the crowd.

I look for her a thousand times.
   Suddenly, turning my head, I see her appear
   where the lantern light is dim.

Being a professional calligrapher

Zhang Sen is scathing about those calligraphers he regards as 'amateurs' posing as professionals. Unlike them, he refuses to stage one-man shows. Since the quality of his calligraphy stands out in group exhibitions and his

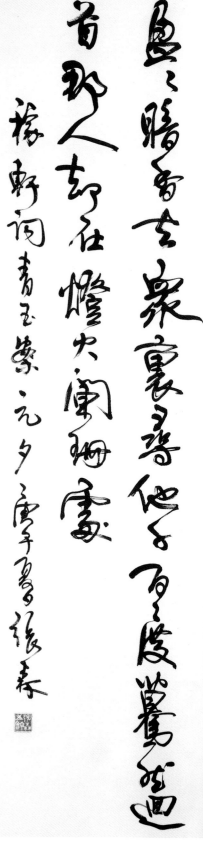

114 Zhang Sen's rendering of Xin Qiji's sensuously evocative poem *The Evening of the Lantern Festival.*

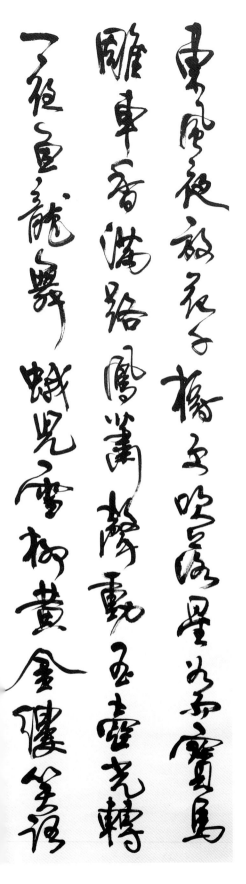

works receive a steady flow of favourable press comment, he feels he does not need to pay out for needless publicity. For the same reason, he refuses to pay to have his name included in the numerous directories of leading modern calligraphers.

He was delighted by an auction of calligraphy that took place in Guangzhou in 1994. The only pieces in it by contemporary calligraphers were by Qi Gong, who at the time was chairman of the Chinese Calligraphers' Association, and by himself. The volume of sales of his books are another indication of Zhang Sen's popularity. Since its publication in 1990, his calligraphic version of the much-loved description by the Tang poet Wang Bo (649–676) of a pavilion by the river at Nanchang in Jiangxi province, entitled *The Preface on the Pavilion of the Prince of Teng* (*Teng Wang Ge Xu*), has sold 33,000 copies. A similar edition of the poem *The Yue Yang Pagoda* (1996) has sold 8,000 copies.

In 1997 Zhang Sen collaborated with four other Chinese calligraphers to reproduce *The Thousand Character Essay* in five different styles of seal script. The text was composed in the early sixth century by Zhou Xingzi on the basis of characters written by Wang Xizhi (303–361), China's most famous calligrapher. Zhou arranged these into a lucid essay of just 1,000 characters, none of which he used more than once. His 250 rhyming sentences, which cover an extraordinary range of subjects, have long been popular as a guide to self-improvement and good conduct. At the time of writing, the 1997 version of the text has sold 10,000 copies; in addition, two collections of Zhang Sen's works published in 1992 and 1998 have sold 3,000 and 4,000 copies respectively. The print runs are impressive by Western standards, but these publications do not generate very much revenue for Zhang Sen himself.

Zhang Sen's reputation as a calligrapher ensures that he receives numerous invitations to the official openings of exhibitions and of new shops, offices and buildings. On these occasions he is invariably expected to write out a few of his very distinctive characters either in a guest book, as a message of congratulations on the success of the event, or perhaps in the form of best wishes for a new enterprise.

Through his attendance at such gatherings he is given a wide range of commissions to provide not only calligraphy for shop signs and the names of public or commercial buildings, but also titles of television programmes, album covers, commemorative medals, even logos for both Chinese and international companies. In 1999 he was asked to design a Chinese logo for the Dresdner Bank, whose main office in China is located in Shanghai's Jin Mao Tower (at that time the tallest building in the country).

Dozens of historical and scenic sites across China are graced by Zhang Sen's calligraphy. They include the Jade Buddha and Longhua Temples in Shanghai, a fine Ming building in Hangzhou, the island of Gulanyu in Xiamen, and the most famous gate in the western section of the Great Wall, the Jia Yu Guan. There are also inscriptions by Zhang Sen at the Temple of Confucius in Qufu in Shandong province and on the Sanjing Mountain in Jiangxi province, famous for its Daoist temples, dangerous peaks and magical cloud effects.

Some businesspeople have attempted to exploit Zhang Sen's calligraphy under false pretences. For example, a Chinese teapot maker was discovered to have forged Zhang Sen's calligraphy on pots in order to sell them at more than US$150 apiece. On the one hand, Zhang Sen is annoyed by such flagrant appropriation of his work; on the other, he feels rather flattered that his calligraphy is in such demand that it is being copied for sale at high prices, even at fairly remote tourist venues.

In Shanghai itself, Zhang Sen is vice-president of both the Calligraphers' Association and the Aesthetics Association (a forum in which artists and academics discuss theoretical aspects of the arts). At national level, he is one of the key people involved in China's efforts to promote the teaching of calligraphy and to raise standards within the art. Since 1988 Zhang Sen has also been one of the directors of the Chinese Calligraphers' Association, and in 1989 he was appointed a member of its recommendation committee. These roles enable him to keep in close touch with developments in traditional styles of calligraphy across the country. His own work is frequently exhibited abroad. Since 1984 he has visited Japan seven times. He has also travelled to Korea, Hong Kong, Singapore, France and Germany in connection with exhibitions featuring his calligraphy.

People admire Zhang Sen's success and like the unpretentious way in which he talks about the importance of art and beauty. When they hear him tell interviewers, 'People who understand calligraphy don't buy it, and those who buy it don't understand it,' they are amused by his audacity even if they do not believe what he says.

Zhang Sen recognizes the deep desire of the well-educated younger generation to explore the pleasures of calligraphy for themselves, and in doing so to embrace their rich cultural heritage at a time when the modernization of China is increasingly isolating them from it. He meets this need by presenting quotations from the Chinese classics which have 'magic' in their words, beautifully written in the fresh styles of script that he has made his own.

LIU ZENGFU
1932–

The scholar-calligrapher

115 Here Liu Zengfu is pictured in his study, in 1999, with his daughter Liu Jia, who is following in her father's footsteps by studying the Chinese classics and calligraphy.

Among contemporary Neo-Classical calligraphers, Liu Zengfu is one of those most firmly positioned in the classical, scholarly tradition. How this came about is a curious tale of family connections, ill health and a quirk of the Cultural Revolution.

A very unusual education

Liu has been greatly influenced by his grandfather, Liu Yizheng (1880–1956), a renowned scholar of Chinese history who also knew an enormous amount about the rest of the world. In addition, he was a highly talented calligrapher, known for his authoritative, scholarly style. As a child, Liu suffered persistent ill health and was therefore unable to go to school. Instead, he was taught at home by his grandfather. He began studying calligraphy at the tender age of four. While precocious in his achievements, he was so overawed by his grandfather's talent that for a long time he found great difficulty in developing his own skills.

Through his grandfather, Liu met most of the cultural luminaries of the day and nearly all of China's leading calligraphers, including Shen Yinmo (pp. 67–73), who is widely regarded as having been one of the best calligraphers of the twentieth century. As a result, he received a more thorough grounding in Chinese culture than almost anyone else of his age.

After the Communist takeover in 1949, Liu's grandfather held a privileged position in Shanghai, primarily because he was greatly revered by Marshal Chen Yi (pp. 91–9), the city's new mayor. One of Chen Yi's early decisions as mayor was to appoint Liu Yizheng to a prominent post in the newly created Cultural Administration Office. Among other things, this organization was tasked with setting up a new museum of Chinese art and a library of mainly Chinese books, neither of which had existed in the old International Settlement. Chen Yi would frequently visit Liu Yizheng in his office to talk to him about poetry and the arts in general. After his friend became sick in his old age, Chen Yi used to send him traditional gifts of money each autumn festival, even though he was in no financial difficulty.

It was only after his grandfather's death in 1956 that Liu Zengfu began to practise his calligraphy seriously. By 1962 he had made such good progress that Shen Yinmo agreed to become his teacher (see fig. 17 on p. 26).

In his lessons with Shen over the next five years Liu was taught running script and learned such techniques as getting the right pressure on the brush, embedding the ink deeply into the paper and shaping characters correctly. But despite his best efforts, he knew that he was still too ebullient, 'like a young horse without reins'.

In 1962, at some thirty years of age, Liu was at last fit enough to look for work. His first job was a part-time one, teaching the rudiments of calligraphy to youngsters at the Young People's Palace. After a year he switched over to teaching the traditional board game *weiqi* (better known in the West by its Japanese name of Go), at which he was a first-rate player. By 1965 his health had improved still further and he was sent to teach at a middle school in Shanghai.

When Mao launched his Cultural Revolution the following year, some of the teachers at the school were badly beaten by their pupils. But Liu, perhaps because little was known about him, was left alone, which is extraordinary, given his cultured family background. Soon the school closed down and most of the students were sent to the countryside to 'learn from the peasants'. Since everyone seemed to have forgotten about Liu, he settled down quietly at home to continue his study of the Chinese classics. Like so many others, he sought solace by practising his calligraphy.

In 1970, when the Cultural Revolution was still far from over, Premier Zhou Enlai made it known to a number of his friends that he felt China urgently needed to cultivate young people to replace China's older generation of scholars, who were rapidly dying off – their demise hastened, in many cases, by the terrible events of the Cultural Revolution. Encouraged by Wang Qingzhen, the head of the Shanghai Museum, Liu decided to intensify his study of China's ancient oracle bones, a subject on which he was already quite knowledgeable.

Finding his efforts somewhat thwarted by the fact that nearly all the academic institutions were still closed, once again Liu made his best progress working at home. Six years later, in 1976, he completed his paper. In it he boldly challenged the views of Guo Moruo (pp. 80–90), who had been president of the Academy of Sciences for more than twenty-five years, on the meaning of a certain phrase that appeared in the oracle-bone script. Before the paper was published, Liu again took up teaching Go, this time as a top coach for the Shanghai Sports Council.

The return of the classics

Only after Deng Xiaoping's return to power in 1978 did Chinese universities feel that they could again start recruiting academic staff to teach

116 Liu wrote out this couplet by his grandfather, Liu Yizheng, in 1996. Its enigmatic content can be read as follows:

*Great talent will always show through,
Like the brightness of the Milky Way,
cascading out of a clear sky.*

classical Chinese. When, in the same year, Shanghai's Fudan University decided to appoint a young lecturer to teach ancient Chinese and oracle-bone script, the only candidate for the position was Liu, who was now forty-six years old.

Although calligraphy was not taught at Fudan, there was considerable interest in the subject. Liu was amply qualified to teach calligraphy at a high level, having worked almost exclusively with a brush, rather than a fountain pen or ballpoint. Indeed, his skill was so impressive that in 1978 his work was awarded first prize at an exhibition in Hong Kong, in competition with many of the leading calligraphers from both Hong Kong and Shanghai. By 1980 he had been invited to teach calligraphy at one of Fudan University's associate colleges.

In the course of his university career, Liu has proved himself to be a prolific scholar of Chinese culture. He has published many books on his grandfather, and on various aspects of the classical Chinese language. In 1995 he became a full professor.

Liu remains passionate about the need for young people to understand their national culture. Indeed, one of his favourite seals bears the words 'The Pro-China Group'. He also believes deeply that people must take responsibility for their own actions and show benevolence in their dealings with others. He therefore attaches great importance to 'gentlemanly behaviour', a concept succinctly expressed in these lines from the *Li Ji* (the 'Book of Rites') compiled by disciples of Confucius some time before 200 BC, which Liu wrote out in 1996:

He who diligently seeks knowledge,
    yet remains modest about what he knows.
He who does virtuous deeds,
    yet never tires of doing so,
That is whom we can call a true gentleman.

Liu retains a great admiration, indeed almost a veneration, for his grandfather, Liu Yizheng. He particularly likes the couplet his grandfather composed by combining one line from a poem by Du Fu (712–770) and another from a poem by Liu Chang (1019–69). Owing to the complexities of the classical Chinese language, it is possible to interpret this couplet in several different ways. One way in which it can be read is shown opposite, under the illustration of Liu's own calligraphic version of his grandfather's poem (fig. 116). However, it is equally possible to take the piece to mean that within the vastness of nature there is space enough for everyone to find his place.

205

Through his long association with Shen Yinmo, Liu learned a great deal about the history and theory of calligraphy, and over the past twenty-five years he has conducted a prodigious amount of research on the subject. In 1985 he collaborated with his friend Zhang Sen (pp. 195–202) on the writing of a textbook entitled *A Basic Knowledge of Clerical Script*, which has sold over 150,000 copies since its publication. In 1999 Liu summarized much of this work in *College Calligraphy*, the first university-level textbook on the subject to be written by a mainland scholar since 1949.

His research into Chinese calligraphers of the nineteenth and twentieth centuries has been published in hundreds of monographs in China. In Japan these publications have appeared more systematically in *Shin Sho Kan*, the leading Japanese journal on calligraphy, under the series title 'An Outline of Modern Chinese Calligraphy'.

In 1992 Liu spent six months at Tsukuba University in Tokyo, which has a large calligraphy department where students can work their way up to doctorate level in the subject. Since then, many Japanese students have come to study under him at Fudan University, and in 1998 he returned for a further spell of teaching in Tokyo. Liu admires the enthusiasm of his Japanese students for the Chinese classics. At the same time he has high expectations of them, demanding that they develop their technique in keeping with the Chinese calligraphic tradition of injecting deep meaning into the content of their work.

Liu is well known not only in Japan but also in Hong Kong, where he is held in high regard for both his calligraphy and his extensive knowledge of the classics. Between 1993 and 1995 he was invited three times to lecture on these subjects at universities in Hong Kong.

A scholarly script

All Liu's calligraphy has a distinctly scholarly air about it. He feels that his best work is that done in either clerical script or running script. He was taught the former by his grandfather, whose own style was characterized by its strength and scholarly grandeur, and the latter by Shen Yinmo. In both of these scripts Liu tends to use a thick brush. He feels that in recent years he has been able to make the structure of his characters freer, and his brushwork has become less restrained and so more energetic (fig. 117). His clerical script is now informed by a deep knowledge of the ancient oracle-bone script, giving it a slightly naïve quality.

Whatever the script in which it is written, Liu's work displays evidence of the secret he learned from Shen Yinmo of carefully controlling the flow of ink from the brush onto the paper, even when the brush is moving quite

117 In 2000, Liu wrote out this classical poem by Wang Wei (701–761), which describes the magnificence of the landscape in western China:

From the vast desert, a single thread of smoke rises up into the Heavens, While beyond the great winding river, the round setting sun descends into the Earth.

fast. This technique ensures that each individual stroke has depth and lustre, and does not suddenly turn dry, allowing Liu to achieve his objective of producing calligraphy that is 'bright, like a fish in clear water'.

Selecting just the right content is another key element in the creation of a successful piece of calligraphy. Whereas his grandfather had the ability to compose original poems in the style of past masters, Liu's own poetry, despite his study of the classics, has little more than a classical flavour. Instead, what he does to great effect is draw on his knowledge of the rich repertoire of classical Chinese poetry and literature. As well as finding elegant and apt quotations through which to project his views and moods, he cleverly combines verses from different poems into new couplets or changes a particular word to give a couplet a whole new meaning.

Liu's work not only stresses his belief in the importance of Confucian values, but is often lyrical and romantic in tone. He has always loved music and enjoyed the delights of the countryside. He wrote out the following poem by Jiang Kui (*c.*1155–*c.*1221) after visiting one of the impressive bridges near Suzhou in 1995 (fig. 118):

> *I composed a new verse*
> *with gentle, graceful rhythms.*
> *Xiao Hong sang it softly*
> *to the tune of my flute.*
> *By the time the music was over,*
> *we had come to the end of the Pine Hill road.*
> *As we looked back, the fourteen-arched bridge*
> *had already disappeared in the evening mist.*

Liu's burgeoning reputation abroad has brought him some interesting commissions within China. One of them was to rewrite the two panels of calligraphy that decorate a historic pavilion on the banks of the Slender West Lake at Yangzhou. It was the first time the panels had been replaced in more than 200 years, and the couplet concerned was one by the Qian Long emperor (1736–95). Another commission was to provide a calligraphic inscription for the gate to the South Mountain Garden in Zhenjiang, a location close to Liu's heart as the place where his grandfather is buried and where one of his favourite calligraphers, Mi Fu (see p. 21), once lived. At the request of the mayor of the town, the two sentences that Liu wrote out were from a poem by the distinguished Qing dynasty calligrapher Da Jiangshang (1623–92).

Since he won the prize in Hong Kong in 1978, Liu's calligraphy has been exhibited a number of times: for example, in Singapore in 1986, at the

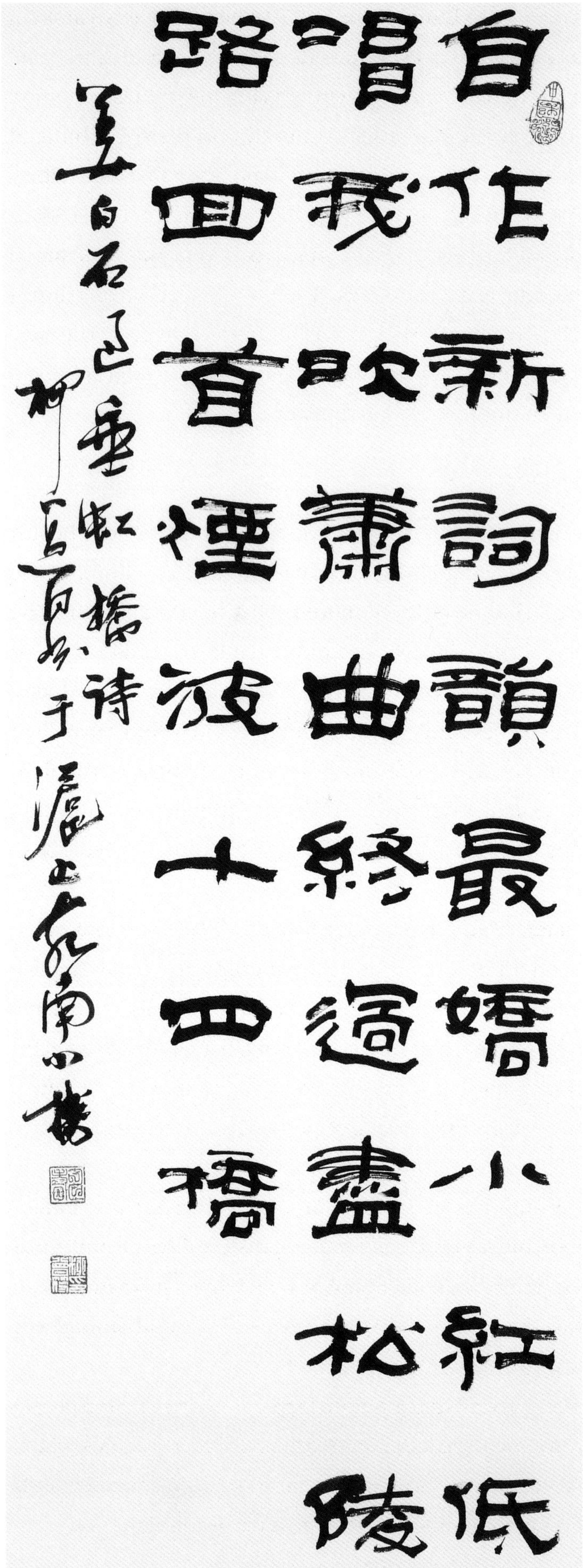

自作新詞韻最嬌
小紅低唱我吹簫
曲終過盡松陵路
回首煙波十四橋

姜白石過垂虹詩
於滬上南小樓

118 This poem conveys the calm pleasures of poetry, music and travelling with a female companion.

208

British Museum in 1996, in Bangkok in 1997 (when he was awarded a gold prize), and also on various occasions in both Osaka and Shanghai.

In addition, Liu has been instrumental in reviving the Chinese tradition of erecting 'forests' of inscriptions. The first new one of these in China, at Zhenjiang, is being built at a cost equivalent to some two and a half million US dollars. It is being modelled on a long-established forest of inscriptions at Xian that features a large number of engraved stone pillars, some of which bear the sole surviving examples of the work of some of China's greatest calligraphers of the past. In sharp contrast, however, the new 'forest' will be made up of works by thirty of the leading calligraphers of today, among them Zhang Sen and Liu himself.

Irony and retirement

Liu's success story is marked by a certain irony in that it was poor health that secured him his excellent classical education in the tradition of the scholar-calligrapher. Had he enjoyed more robust health as a child, he would have attended school in the normal way and so would not have been taught by his illustrious grandfather, Liu Yizheng – and indeed may not have studied the classics at all. Nor, no doubt, would he have benefited from such close contact with other major cultural figures of the day. Moreover, had his classical education been a conventional one, Liu would probably have found himself in difficulty during the Cultural Revolution, if not earlier.

Since his retirement from Fudan University in 1998, Liu has lived in a comfortable apartment in one of the 1920s-built houses that line the leafy lanes of the older part of the city. Here he continues to practise his calligraphy, which he senses is now achieving the assuredness and maturity of style to which he has so long aspired. At last, he says, 'my hand is obeying my heart – reflecting moods of happiness, anger, tranquillity and sorrow.'

Although Liu still finds time to serve as director of the Shanghai Calligraphers' Association, and to teach a few students, these days he puts most of his effort into his writings on calligraphy, which appear frequently in such publications as the weekly *Calligraphy Guide Paper* and Shanghai's leading daily newspaper, *Wen Hui Bao*.

Over the past twenty years Liu has taught large numbers of young people – among them his own teenage daughter (see fig. 115) – the richness of the Chinese calligraphic tradition, and in particular the value of complementing artistic execution with wisdom and significance of content.

HAN YU

1931–

An astute observer of line and foible

Han Yu is something of a cult figure among the Chinese intelligentsia. He has risen from acute poverty to become one of China's most cerebral cartoonists and a writer renowned for the perceptiveness of his observations, which he presents in elegantly simple language. The flowing lines of his calligraphy reveal the strength of a man who has endured much hardship, but who is calmly self-confident in expressing his feelings.

An early distaste for rules

Han Yu's parents were peasants. He therefore suffered extreme hardship as a child. Fortunately, not far from where the family lived in Shandong province there was a local school where he was able to receive a basic education free of charge. Here, like all the other children at the school, Han Yu learned to read and write. The pupils were taught writing by the traditional method: first by tracing individual characters, then by writing them out from copybooks. Han Yu loved calligraphy, but hated these repetitive exercises, which even then he felt destroyed his creative spirit. From the outset, he rejected the rules and wrote his characters in a very free style.

119 Han Yu excels as a writer, cartoonist, painter and calligrapher, yet is disarmingly modest about his talents.

The teacher would show his displeasure at this approach by marking Han Yu's exercise sheets with heavy crosses. He was equally displeased when the eleven-year-old Han Yu began spending his evenings performing with a local Chinese opera troupe. His involvement with the troupe lasted for no more than two or three years, but during that time the graceful movements and gestures of the singers in their silk costumes made Han Yu aware of the beauty of flowing lines, while the stories acted out in the operas sparked in him an interest in the foibles of human behaviour.

When Han Yu was fourteen his free education came to an end and he was sent to work in a shop as a porter, carrying heavy merchandise about. Though relieved to have been liberated from the disapproval of his schoolmaster, he soon realized that if he was to escape from the misery of poverty he would have to educate himself. This decision led him to the local library, which was already (in 1946/7) in the hands of the Communists. The new librarians would lend him recently acquired, freshly printed editions of the works of Marx and Lenin, but were largely unable to help him satisfy his intellectual curiosity by providing books on other subjects. Nonetheless, he managed to get hold of an old Chinese encyclopaedic dictionary, which was to become both his tutor and his friend. He keeps a copy of it by his side to this day.

The staff at the library soon grew fond of this bright young lad. When he was seventeen, they found him a job etching colour plates in the printing department of the local Cultural Bureau. Before long Han Yu discovered that he had a talent for painting, which he was able to develop rapidly over the next few years. In the 1950s he began producing bold propaganda posters in praise of China's economic development under the Communist Party. However, he much preferred some of his other tasks, such as creating traditional folk paintings of cheerful peasants, illustrating storybooks and devising subtly humorous political cartoons. By the early 1960s, so well known was he as an artist and cartoonist that his future second wife had been an admirer of his work even before she met him.

When the Cultural Revolution got under way in 1966, Han Yu was working in the Hebei Provincial Cultural Bureau, where he was severely criticized for the traditional style of his art and his 'feudal' outlook. Towards the end of that year, for a few days all the big-character posters at the bureau were devoted exclusively to criticism of him. It was a traumatic period. After a while, the Red Guards transferred their attention to others and life gradually became a little easier for Han Yu. Nevertheless, he continued to feel vulnerable, knowing that at heart he really was a 'Rightist', even though he had not yet been specifically condemned as such.

By the early 1970s the acute disruption generated by the Cultural Revolution was over. Even so, there was virtually no work to be done at the bureau, as new policies had not yet been formulated. Han Yu was therefore able to spend more of his time at his home in a village outside Shijiazhuang, away from the political excesses of city life. During this period he turned to painting watercolours of Chinese operas, recalling the happier days of his childhood. His style was influenced by the strong, simple images he had used in his cartoons. The result was a series of vibrantly coloured paintings that had a rustic, even naïve, quality, but were in tune with modern taste.

Cartoons and impressionism

With so much free time on his hands, Han Yu began to take a greater interest in calligraphy, though at this stage only as an adjunct to his painting. In his twenties and thirties he had been a passionate admirer of Yu Youren (see pp. 22–3), whose fine-lined calligraphy had a childlike purity about it. Despite this attraction, he decided against copying Yu's work. He felt that, even at his best, he would never be more than one of the 'little Yu Yourens'.

Instead, he decided to base the development of his own calligraphic style on the 'impressions' he received from the work of Yu Youren and other calligraphers he admired.

The lack of work during this period also gave Han Yu the opportunity to make several trips to Beijing. One of the people he was most keen to meet there was the former stage designer Zhang Zhengyu (pp. 119–24), who had been breathing new life into traditional calligraphy for more than a decade. The two artists got along very well.

In 1976 Zhang introduced Han Yu to Huang Miaozi (pp. 172–81), who had himself been a cartoonist in his youth and who at that time had not long been released after his seven years' imprisonment. Zhang died later the same year, but Huang and Han Yu remain good friends to this day and have a great respect for each other's work. Huang affectionately describes his friend as the 'Old Potato', a reference to Han Yu's large forehead and still somewhat rustic appearance.

Han Yu had less time to spare after 1975. First he was allocated a post teaching art in a local secondary school, then in 1982 he joined the teaching staff at the Hebei Provincial Academy of Art in Shijiazhuang, where he continued to develop his painting. He also created a series of cartoons that were much more humorous and satirical than any he had done before. A famous Japanese cartoonist so admired them that he invited Han Yu to go and live in Japan. Han Yu declined, feeling that living overseas was 'more than he could cope with'. However, most of the cartoons he produced during the 1980s were not published until 1995, by which time China's political climate had become more stable.

Subtlety and freshness

Han Yu still lives in the compound of the Academy on the fringes of Shijiazhuang. The blocks of apartments in which the staff are housed are neither attractive nor well maintained. Nevertheless, the money Han Yu has made from the sale of his works has enabled him and his second wife to create a home that is a tasteful oasis of orderly calm. Their living room is presided over by a fine painting of a black cat that was a gift from Zhang Zhengyu and is just the sort of painting that got Zhang into trouble during the Cultural Revolution. It is in his studio-cum-library that Han Yu settles down to write his articles, draw his cartoons and create his calligraphy.

Although Han Yu often dresses quite smartly, in the heat of summer he tends to revert to the kind of cotton singlet and shorts he wore when young, thus remaining true to his belief that intellectuals do not have to 'dress up' in order to fulfil their elevated role in life.

120 As with much of Han Yu's work, this couplet, *Falling Leaves*, is enigmatic. Its meaning can be interpreted in various ways.

As the years have gone by, Han Yu has become increasingly concerned about maintaining his creativity. When he was younger he was careful to avoid modelling the style of his calligraphy on that of earlier masters. In more recent years, however, he has sought inspiration from a wide range of sources. These include not only the rubbings made from China's ancient stone engravings, but also the works of contemporary calligraphers, signboards on the street, a variety of trades and crafts, children's calligraphy, and in one instance even notices written by a semi-literate mail-room worker he knew at the Academy.

Whatever it is that catches Han Yu's eye, he does not copy it down, for fear of becoming an artistic 'photocopier' and thus losing his powers of creativity. As with the works of the great masters, he lets the points that most fascinate him sink deep into his mind, where they can mingle with his own personality, experience and interests. By the time they appear in his art, they have been transformed into something very different from the original impression that was made on him. His approach is not unlike that of a Western fashion designer who draws inspiration from the eye-catching combinations of clothing that teenagers wear on the streets.

Han Yu insists that calligraphy should be fun. It should, he says, give pleasure to the artist while at the same time producing beautiful results that visibly convey his feelings. But pleasure does not always come easily to the artist. Han Yu will often shut himself away in his study for hours at a time as he strives to perfect a piece of calligraphy.

This is the antithesis of the standard approach. Many traditional calligraphers, who by definition have practised in a disciplined way for many years, devote most of their time to composing a piece of calligraphy in their head before committing it to paper. Conversely, Han Yu values the freshness of spontaneous inspiration and believes that the freedom of style he nurtured as a cartoonist helps him to remain innovative in his calligraphy. However, he often finds himself unable to achieve the effect he is seeking at the first attempt. He is ruthless in destroying anything that does not fully satisfy him.

There is often an intriguing ambiguity in Han Yu's work. A good example of this is to be found in his couplet *Falling Leaves* (fig. 120), which he wrote out in 1993:

The west wind blows, the water flows.
The leaves fall on Chang'an.

At one level the words simply evoke autumn in China's ancient capital of Chang'an (now known as Xian). That is what Han Yu himself claims his

213

couplet is about. However, other Chinese have read much more into it:

The autumn wind comes from the West
and, like the river flowing,
it shows that time is running out.

The leaves fall on Chang'an,
where, like earlier dynasties that have ruled there,
they rot away.

It is equally possible to interpret the couplet in other ways. It can be seen as a philosophical statement, as a general observation on history, or as a commentary on a specific moment in China's history.

Those examples of Han Yu's calligraphy that do meet with his approval, and therefore survive, bring to mind the description of calligraphy as the art of making 'the brush dance and the ink sing'. The structure of his characters is loose, and the fluidity of his brushstrokes creates such a sense of depth that frequently one is indeed reminded of a dancer in motion. This impression is reinforced by his skill in making his ink flow out from the brushstroke in an extraordinary range of textures that could be said to 'give voice' to his characters.

Another way in which Han Yu's approach differs from that of other calligraphers is that he seldom produces calligraphy on request. On the rare occasions when he does work to commission, the result tends to have an almost palpable feeling of obligation about it. As an example, one might cite the piece he was invited to contribute to a local exhibition to mark the centenary of Mao's birth in 1994. The fifty or so characters of which it is comprised lack visual excitement. His best works are entirely different in feel and contain either images that intrigue him or sentiments intended to cheer and inspire.

In 1996, three years after writing *Falling Leaves*, Han Yu created two pieces of calligraphy that summed up his overall view of life. The first reflects his belief that with the right outlook and preparation one can achieve surprising things. To make the point, he selected a couplet from *Rhyme-Prose on Literature*, the best-known work by the Han dynasty poet Lu Ji (261–303). Taken from a passage that describes the practice of meditating before writing, it translates as:

Then, at full gallop your spirit can
reach the limits of the cosmos.
And your mind, buoyed with inspiration, will now
soar to hitherto insurmountable heights.

121 This couplet, by Han Yu himself, is about keeping things in perspective, which he has often found the need to do over the years.

The second piece (fig. 121) underlines the importance Han Yu attaches to seeing life in terms of the 'bigger picture'. Here the words are his own:

If you can rise up towards the sun,
and go beyond the clouds,
You will be able to see all the world
in perspective.

Those who have read Han Yu's articles or studied his calligraphy feel that these two pairs of scrolls reflect his own achievements very well.

Han Yu is greatly admired in Chinese literary circles. His articles are relished for their clarity of language and the acuteness of their observations. However, he claims to be unable to write good poems, citing this as one reason why he so often writes out the poetry of others. Nevertheless, when he does compose his own pieces they have a strong classical flavour.

Han Yu is an outstanding example of someone whose situation has been transformed for the better through firm resolve and self-education. He has pulled himself up out of poverty to the prestige of earning the acclaim of the intelligentsia. Both the astuteness of his views and the subtlety with which he presents them in his writings and cartoons retain an enduring freshness. His clarity of vision and depth of experience have enabled him to develop a form of Neo-Classical calligraphy that excites not simply because of its beauty and strength, but also through the meaning of his words. Han Yu's work is an innovative continuation of the Grand Tradition.

Detail of fig. 120

SA BENJIE

1948–

The subtle explorer of perceptions

Sa Benjie is one of the most humane and imaginative members of China's newer generation of calligraphers. In his works he subtly explores human perceptions and philosophizes on matters that reflect the mood of the day. Despite his modern outlook, his office at Rong Bao Zhai in Beijing, where he is the leading authority on painting and calligraphy, has the traditional look of a scholar's studio. Similarly traditional is Sa's mode of dress. He has not adopted the Western styles now so fashionable in China, but prefers chic variants of the kind of clothes Chinese scholars used to wear.

122 Sa Benjie in his office

The making of a calligrapher

In certain respects, the scholarly status that Sa has attained is similar to that held by some of his ancestors. However, he arrived at this point by a rather different route. Unlike their prosperous forebears, Sa's parents both came from the ranks of the impoverished gentry. Nevertheless, they managed to get him into one of the best schools in Beijing. And every night, after he had finished his homework, his mother would give him extra tuition in calligraphy.

Sa was one of the most promising pupils at his school, which led to his meeting Premier Zhou Enlai and Marshal Chen Yi (pp. 91–9). These encounters gave him a comforting sense of being connected with China's new 'aristocracy'. By the time he reached secondary school, however, the mood in China had changed radically. Simply because of his gentrified family background, he was not allowed to join the Young Communist League.

Matters were made much worse when, in 1965, Sa disclosed to some of his fellow students what he had found out about China's recent atomic bomb testing from reading a 'confidential' news bulletin in his mother's office. As a result, first he was made to undergo the indignity of public self-criticism, then he was expelled from the Students' Union. Being treated in this way convinced him that he should steer clear of politics in future. But this was easier said than done.

The Cultural Revolution wrecked Sa's chances of going to university. In 1968 he was one of the many pre-university students packed off to the

countryside in order to 'learn from the peasants'. Dumped in a harrowingly poor village, Sa sought to ease his anguish by practising his calligraphy. This went some way towards reassuring him that despite his isolation he still belonged to a cultured world. The locals thought he was mad. But because the texts he was copying out were from *The Thoughts of Chairman Mao* and Mao's poems, no one could attack him on the grounds that his attitude was politically incorrect.

After three years he was allowed to join his elderly mother, who had been sent to a cadre school belonging to the Ministry of Culture near Tianjin. The place was packed with artists and intellectuals. There Sa met Wang Xiaju, a distinguished calligrapher, who agreed to become his tutor. At first Sa was frustrated by Wang's strict methods, but gradually it became clear to him what his new master was trying to achieve. After insisting that Sa study closely the rules of calligraphy, Wang showed him how to inject flexibility into his work. Only when he was satisfied with his progress in these two areas did Wang let Sa use calligraphy to convey his own personality and feelings.

Having spent two years at the cadre school in Tianjin, Sa then spent another five working in a factory connected with the Ministry of Culture. In 1978 his connection with the Ministry led to his being given a job at Beijing's principal art shop and gallery, Rong Bao Zhai, dealing with the purchase and sale of old Chinese paintings and calligraphy. At thirty years of age, this was one of the happiest moments in Sa's life. At Rong Bao Zhai he would have a chance to study art, to see a steady flow of the works of the masters, both ancient and modern, and to develop his own calligraphic skills. This opportunity, he felt, would make up for the fact that he had been denied his university education.

After years of study, Sa came to the conclusion that the artists whose calligraphy he admired most were Yu Youren (1879–1964), Li Shutong (1880–1942) and Qi Baishi (1863–1957). To him, their works did not appear 'contrived', but displayed an innocence of inspiration that gave them freshness and vitality.

The more Sa worked on his calligraphy, the more he came to believe that the essence of the art lay not in matters of style, rules or composition, but in the artist's exploration of his own feelings – about the world, about society and about himself. This conviction was crystallized in his mind by the tragic events in Tiananmen Square on the night of 4 June 1989. From that time onwards he began to develop a form of expression that was more personal and reflective. Although all his own poems and prose contain classical elements, they are essentially modern in tone. They have been an important force in shaping his calligraphic style.

In the early 1990s Sa embarked on the development of some innovative writing and calligraphic styles in order to express himself even more fully. In both the content and the composition of his work, he began combining elements of false naivety with contrasting elements that were highly sophisticated. This was a gradual process, however. Unlike many of his peers, Sa rarely puts brush to paper unless he has some new thought that he wishes to convey.

One thing at this time that did spur him into producing a new piece was the openness and honesty of observations made by his young daughter. In 1993 he wrote a horizontal scroll entitled *A Talk between Friends*, in which he noted:

> *We have discussed all manner of things*
> > *that have happened since the beginning of history.*
> *We have spoken to each other without fear of retribution.*
> *Yet those who are the boldest,*
> > *are those who speak with the directness of a child.*

Furniture calligraphy

Sa then began to build on the insight he had gained from studying the late compositions of Qi Baishi, in which painting and calligraphy work together to tell a story. Through his close association with Wang Shixiang (pp. 153–61), the great scholar and collector of Chinese furniture, Sa had become fascinated by the history of individual pieces of furniture. He began to formulate the notion that each item of furniture developed a 'personality' of its own, and that this could be used as a metaphor for the thoughts and actions of human beings.

Among Wang's collection was an elegant Ming scroll table (which is illustrated in his classic books on Ming furniture), whose recent history seemed curiously to parallel events in his own life. In 1994 this inspired Sa to create his first piece of 'furniture calligraphy', *A Fable about a Table* (fig. 129). In very moving language he recounts the history of the table from the moment Wang rescued it from being destroyed in the 1950s to the time when he donated it to the Shanghai Museum in the 1990s. The calligraphy that tells the story is spread over a painted silhouette of the table itself.

The same year, Sa's follow-up to this piece was a series of six delightful compositions featuring Chinese chairs and a stool (figs 123–8). He uses these sometimes to comment on relationships within a family and some-times to muse on other matters. In each case the item of furniture looks

LEFT TO RIGHT, FROM TOP:

123 *What a Family!*
124 *Father and Son*
125 *Stepmother and Child*
126 *Seats of History*
127 *The Golden Wedding Photo*
128 *Sit and Contemplate*

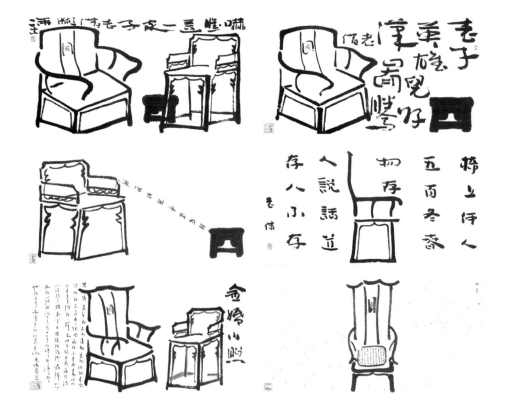

the part it is playing. The first piece in the series depicts the father's chair, the mother's chair and the son's stool and is accompanied by the exclamation 'What a family!'. The second picture, which shows the father's chair and the stool, bears the inscription: 'The father is a hero, the son a brave little fellow.'

In the next composition the mother has her say, in the form of a well-known phrase from a Beijing opera: 'How difficult relationships can be! It is hard for a stepmother to bring up a naughty boy.'

129 *A Fable about a Table*

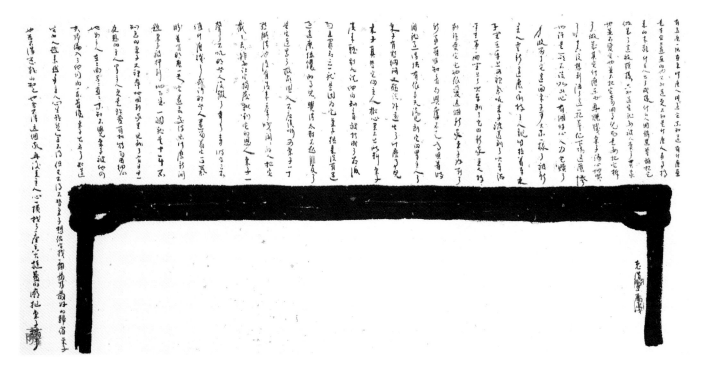

As the series progresses, Sa's tone becomes more reflective. It is in this mood that, in the fourth piece, he reflects on the passage of time.

Someone sat on this chair 500 years ago.
As the chair is still here,
    we can imagine that man still talking.
And even though we know he no longer exists,
    what he said remains true.

His penultimate piece, entitled *The Golden Wedding Photo*, includes an image of a 'male' and a 'female' chair, accompanied by a moving poem written in the subtle colloquial style known as *qu*. Few people can match Sa in this particular form of verse.

Details of fig. 127

Before our marriage we had our separate lives.
Since our wedding photo was taken, much has changed.
In a trice, half a century has passed.
It was not easy to share hardship for so long.
Yet we are still who we were.

If we look closely at each other,
    we can vaguely see what we were like
      all those years ago when we were young.
Although we now take another picture that records the ravages of time,
    we have not really changed.
I am still me and you are still you.

The series ends on a note of quiet contemplation, with a piece that Sa claims to have composed 'to cool the heat' of a hot summer's night in 1994:

It was midnight and the world was silent.
When I awoke, I could see nothing
    and my mind was blank.
Suddenly, many strange and extraordinary things occurred to me.
I have never felt so bright or quick-witted.
If you sit on this chair in a Buddhist pose of contemplation,
    you may have the same feeling.

Finding oneself

Towards the end of 1994, which had been a particularly busy and stressful year for Sa, he began experimenting with much larger characters based on a fluid form of seal script. Seeing this as an appropriate style in which to express his wish at that time to be left in peace to do his own work, he wrote out a well-known couplet that declared 'Let someone else fill in the sea. Just leave me alone to get on with building up the mountain.'

Sa has always been interested in matters of perception, especially the wide range of feelings one can experience. This was the theme of a piece he did in early 1995, by which time he was in a calmer frame of mind: 'Once you really sense something, you are exhilarated in feeling and spirit.' A year later, as his thoughts returned to the problems of stress and relaxation, he wrote out a couplet that plays on an old Daoist theme: 'Only when you are not hard-pressed can you achieve a state of cool, inner calm.'

In all three of these pieces Sa followed the convention that both lines of a couplet should have the same number of characters, and that the characters in each vertical line should be of identical size.

For some time, however, Sa had felt that this style of calligraphy was no longer in harmony with his own emotions and ideas. Drawing inspiration from the clerical script of Yi Bingshou (1754–1815), he had found that giving prominence to horizontal lines and dots and using different-sized characters allowed him to introduce greater flexibility into the form of his compositions. He could immediately see that his brushwork had never been so free. To celebrate the fact, in 1995 he wrote out the following couplet (see fig. 32 on pp. 36–7):

Only when you have let yourself sink into complete confusion
can you start to climb back towards clear-mindedness.

As Sa himself points out, these lines can also be read as meaning that 'in a harsh and unfair world, all one can do is shut one's eyes'.

By late 1996 Sa was at a stage where his heightened artistic activity of the past couple of years had been something of a journey of self-discovery. It was at this time that he composed the lines: 'By being an idle man in an empty space, I begin to see myself face to face.' This couplet is an extremely clever play on homonyms, the second line being a reverse reading of the sounds in the first: *Wo jin xian shi, Shi xian jin wo.* It was a device Sa would use again. The piece is written in an open, elongated style of running script that is very relaxed, suggesting that Sa was by no means displeased with the couplet he had composed.

In his next work he returned to the subject of human perception. In the light of his own experience, Sa has come to believe that any profound emotion or sensation is multifaceted, involving several of the senses at once. Similarly, solving a problem usually depends on analysing it from various points of view. His belief in the virtue of perceiving things in a new way is encapsulated in his couplet 'See the tea, eat the ink, rub the pot, taste the book'. In this pair of scrolls Sa chose to focus attention on the message he was conveying by using a remarkably direct style of calligraphy. He used thin, simple lines to form elongated characters, allowing the dryness of his brush to highlight the mood of calm. The characters in each scroll are paired in the traditional manner, but by varying their size he has achieved a subtle visual balance between them, echoing the interplay of the senses dealt with in the text itself.

In Sa's opinion, most of us fail to unwind frequently enough and so rarely, if ever, feel fully at ease with ourselves. Only by 'letting go', he believes, can we appreciate our own value and discover our true identity. Having thought about this for some time, one morning in 1997 he got up very early and, with greater artistic energy than ever before, wrote out with a flourish (on the back of a sheet of Rong Bao Zhai's wrapping paper) eight characters that translate as:

Let yourself go,
put yourself at ease.

This expressed precisely what Sa felt he personally had achieved. He was delighted with the result (fig. 130).

Soon, however, he began to doubt whether he had yet 'found himself'. Towards the end of the year he wrote out a phrase in Beijing dialect: 'I wonder who this really is?' (*Bu zhi zhege shi shei*). As if to underline his change of mood, he wrote this in a new style, using a soft brush to create thick strokes that exaggerate the horizontal structure of the characters. The fragmented lines and tentative brushwork result in a composition of calm elegance that seems to pay homage both to the equilibrium of Yi Bingshou's calligraphy and to the special clarity of Li Shutong's.

No doubt there were a number of factors behind Sa's renewed compulsion to question who he really was. Life at Rong Bao Zhai had changed greatly since his arrival some two decades earlier. It was now a thriving commercial enterprise selling everything from popular items to exceedingly expensive works of art, either directly or through its auctions. Sa's responsibilities had increased considerably, as had his rewards – he had been given a comfortable new apartment within the city and a car of his own. He had also made his first ever trip outside China, to Malaysia and Japan. Only by going to bed early and rising at dawn could he still find time to think and to develop his calligraphy.

In 1998 Sa sent my wife a pair of scrolls that contained an elegant and clever compliment. Their elegance lay in his reference to two types of orchid: one that has a single flower and another that has several. Together, the

130 *Let Yourself Go* is exactly what Sa did when he produced this piece of calligraphy in 1997.

two lines of the couplet can be interpreted as meaning 'You have a quiet and graceful charm. How pleased I am to have met you.' Once again Sa had wittily taken advantage of the peculiarities of spoken Chinese to compose a couplet in which the sounds of the characters that made up the first line were exactly reversed in the second. In terms of the calligraphy itself, this piece marked a further phase in the development of Sa's style: through the use of thin, elongated characters, tightly composed, he had devised a new form of seal script.

Another theme that has long fascinated Sa is one that also preoccupied the French philosopher Jean-Jacques Rousseau – namely, the extent to which people are corrupted by the society in which they live. Sa believes that what we are taught rarely helps us to understand fully the difference

223

between what is true and what is false, or what is beautiful and what is ugly. These things have to be learnt through personal experience of life and society. Unfortunately, by the time we achieve enlightenment we are likely to be advanced in years. He expressed these sentiments in the following couplet, which he wrote in a simple script that has considerable strength despite its thinness of line:

In the first half of my life, I was misled and corrupted
by the ways of civilization;
Only in my middle years have I come to understand
something about truth and beauty.

During the late 1990s Sa also produced some further works in his 'furniture calligraphy' series. The first were small abstract pieces in which he painted the graceful lines and curves of antique Chinese furniture in such a way that they looked like meaningful calligraphy. He then went on to create some large works, in which he achieved a wonderful effect whereby the strong dark 'bones' of his brushstrokes became surrounded by a lighter and softer 'flesh' as a more watery ink oozed into the paper. His interest in developing new ink techniques had come about through working on abstract compositions, where he was not focusing on the relationship between the content and the form of his calligraphy.

Sa does not regard himself as a 'modern' calligrapher, but he does believe that his abstract pieces centred on images of furniture fit squarely into the artistic category of calligraphy. Whereas most traditional calligraphers mount their works as scrolls, Sa likes to let his float within the borders of a dark wooden frame with rounded corners. This type of frame, he feels, echoes the simple elegance of the Ming furniture itself and so helps focus the eye upon the art within it.

Another theme to which Sa returned in the late 1990s was the intriguing subject of human personality and behaviour. Having long felt that the Chinese were obsessively self-controlled, he was taken by the thought that in order to enjoy a sense of equilibrium, one has to achieve a balance between the social need to display restraint and the personal need to 'let go' or 'open up'. This balance gives people the freedom to open up without fear of going too far, knowing that their self-control will always prevent them from doing so. To make this point, Sa wrote out the phrase *Shou de zhu* (meaning the ability to maintain self-control, or the disinclination to 'let oneself go') on a traditional Chinese fan. It was an inspired piece of symbolism, reliant on the fact that a fan can only function when opened up, but can never open up beyond a certain point.

131 *Realization* (2000)

A new realization

Sa then began work on another innovative series, this time on the theme of 'realization', in which he created new characters that conveyed old meanings. The Chinese term for realization is *jue wu*. This particular concept of realization, or awakening, is related to the Buddhist belief that only when there is nothing at all in your mind is the way clear for your spirit to arrive at true understanding. According to Zen Buddhism, if one can achieve absolute calm by letting one's mind become void of all thought, the first thing to break through the 'hole of stillness' will be this sense of realization, its light coming from all directions.

The novelty of Sa's calligraphy lay in the fact that he combined the two characters *jue* and *wu* into one (fig. 131; see also figs 26 and 27 on p. 32). Sa feels that the individual characters at first appear calm and then seem to come to life as you look at them more carefully. Conversely, the combined versions of them are lively at first glance, but become calmer on closer inspection.

Once he had created this device, Sa produced a series of similar pieces, some of which comprise several different combinations of *jue* and *wu*. The point he wanted to make to the viewer was that only when you have been 'awoken' to something that has happened are you able to 'realize' its significance. That is why the two characters are often deeply intertwined in these works.

Sa has also experimented with several variations on this theme. In one work he took an eight-character Chinese phrase that can be translated as either 'The smartest people don't look as if they are' or 'He who seems to be a fool may be wise' and compressed it into four combination characters. In this instance the technique is particularly well suited to the message. Although, on the surface, Sa's new combined characters look strange and unorthodox, in fact they contain a very succinct message.

Although Sa is one of the least prolific calligraphers of his generation, he is one of the most creative. Like his hero Qi Baishi, he has experimented with the interplay between calligraphy and painting, both representational and abstract. He has also created new and subtle forms of calligraphy, which help focus the attention of the viewer on the meaning of the text and the ideas that lie behind it. By introducing into his art his own deep thoughts about perceptions, emotions and self-expression, he has caught the imagination of China's younger generation, who think about life and about themselves in very different terms from their parents. This is Neo-Classicism at its best.

225

8 THE AVANT-GARDE

ZHANG DAWO

1943–

Making the brush fly

132 Zhang Dawo has created a new and distinctive form of abstract art that is deeply rooted in the traditions of Chinese calligraphy.

Zhang Dawo is a mild-mannered cosmopolitan who produces Avant-Garde calligraphic art of great vitality. His work reflects both his upbringing in a cultured family in the early days of New China and his experiences during the Cultural Revolution. Over recent years he has drawn much inspiration from the time he spends in Australia.

From culture to the wilderness

Zhang is descended on his father's side from a line of famous Chinese landscape gardeners and on his mother's from a line of prominent scholars. Both sides of the family were well-to-do and superficially modern: as Zhang puts it, they wore Western suits but clung to traditional values.

Zhang's father was a professor of English, a language he spoke beautifully despite not travelling abroad until he was seventy. He was, however, more successful as a scholar than as a husband. Zhang's parents separated when he was barely three years of age, with the result that much of his early childhood was spent in the care of his grandparents.

From the age of ten until his early teens, Zhang lived in Tianjin with his father, who had been sent there to teach at Nankai University. In Tianjin Zhang took private lessons in calligraphy with the city's two most distinguished practitioners, Li Henian and Wu Yuru. Wu was a leading scholar of the Chinese classics, widely regarded as one of China's best calligraphers of recent centuries.

In the evenings Zhang would be made to sit and paint while his father played the violin. Although he resented it at the time, he now believes that this early experience of absorbing two art forms at the same time has considerably widened his artistic horizons.

By his late teens Zhang was living in Beijing, where he was constantly miserable. Ill-health denied him the grades he required to enter university, adding to the friction that had already built up between him and his authoritarian father. The tension within the household was further aggravated by Zhang's intense dislike of his new stepmother. He became so unhappy that in 1963, shortly after graduating from high school, he volunteered to leave the crowds and comforts of Beijing to begin a new life as a teacher in the virgin lands that were being opened up in north-eastern China.

227

He was sent to Suidong, a small town at the confluence of three of the main rivers in Heilongjiang province. Although life was tough in China's virgin lands, Zhang achieved a degree of inner peace there. He was exhilarated by the great wild expanses of the landscape and by the thrill of outdoor pursuits such as fishing and hunting. For the first time in his life he found himself making real friends. Above all, he had time to read and to think. While continuing his studies in classical literature through the radio broadcasts of China's open university, he also painted, practised his calligraphy and wrote poems about nature.

At the start of the Cultural Revolution in 1966, Zhang's fortunes took a sudden turn for the worse. Back in Beijing the Red Guards started victimizing his father, first vilifying him and then ransacking his house and imprisoning him for being a 'bad element'. Neither did Zhang escape the purges, even though he was living so far away from the capital. Having already been barred from teaching, he, too, was soon imprisoned by the local Red Guards. Luckily, the conditions were not as bad as he had feared. The 'prison' turned out to be no more than a large cowshed, into which his friends were regularly able to pass him small gifts of food and clothing. One event that did leave a scar, however, was the fact that a close friend who had been detained with him committed suicide in the cowshed, using a belt that belonged to Zhang himself.

After eighteen months' imprisonment Zhang was released and assigned to manual labour, in the course of which he acquired a number of practical skills from his fellow workers. The experience also increased his appreciation of the art that is to be seen in nature. He had already learned a great deal from his family about landscape gardening – including how the judicious placement of earth, rocks, water and vegetation can create illusions of depth and variations of texture in a landscape – but it was really through this first serious encounter with manual work that he came to understand for himself the characteristics of earth, wood, stone and water.

Zhang's life brightened up considerably in 1971 when he married his childhood sweetheart, with whom he had recently been reunited. A year later he was allowed to resume teaching. Only in 1979, however, more than two years after the end of the Cultural Revolution, were he and his wife granted permission to return home to Beijing with their two young children.

After so many years 'in the wilderness', Zhang was more than glad to be back in the cultural environment of the capital. Now thirty-six years old, he was desperate to make up for lost time. He wanted to continue his education in the broadest sense, and above all to concentrate on his calligraphy. But at the same time he needed to earn a living. He was lucky enough to find a job teaching calligraphy at one of Beijing's leading secondary schools, and not long afterwards several of his pupils won prizes in the first student calligraphy competition to be held in China since 1949.

Zhang was subsequently assigned to teach calligraphy and literature at the Capital University in Beijing. By then he had become even more interested in the art of calligraphy and was devoting much of his spare time to improving his techniques. After his long years in the north-east, Zhang saw life very differently. He felt a need to express through his art the strong emotions that had been engendered in him not only by recent events, but also by his childhood experiences. At the same time he hoped that his art would go some way towards soothing wounds he knew would never heal. He had already turned for comfort to Zen Buddhism, which stresses the need to elevate the spirit beyond mere worldly concerns.

Creating a new vocabulary

Serendipity played its part in propelling Zhang's search for self-expression in a radically new direction. One day in 1982, he suddenly found himself fascinated by the multi-layered effect that was being created as different densities of ink oozed into an old sheet of calligraphy he was using to clean one of his brushes. This moment marked his entry into the field of modern calligraphy. He has been experimenting with ink techniques ever since.

Zhang worked in isolation on his new style of calligraphy until he met up with kindred spirits during the exhibition of Modernist calligraphy that was held in Beijing in 1985. This was a highly creative stage in the development of contemporary Chinese calligraphy. Zhang's experiments influenced a number of the Modernists, while he drew inspiration from certain of their works.

Within two years he had produced *The Volume (Ce)*, a piece that was highly praised by several critics and is now regarded as one of the seminal works of the early period of the Modernist movement. This composition was inspired by the ancient pictograms that were the earliest form of written Chinese. These used to be drawn on to wooden or bamboo strips, the strips then being sewn together side by side in such a way that they could be rolled up for transport or storage. Zhang's great achievement was to rework the structure of the character *ce* and use the tonalities of his ink to make it seem as if an ancient scroll were being unfurled before our very eyes. It was in this work that he first made his characters look like three-dimensional sculptures – an effect that was to become one of the hallmarks of his work.

In his calligraphy Zhang has been attracted to both the delicacy that can be achieved and the strength of expression that can be conveyed with a brush. From the mid-1980s he experimented for nearly a decade with the sinuous forms referred to as 'worm' or 'bird' scripts. These terms relate to the traditional belief in China that calligraphy originated from man's observation of the trails left by birds, worms and other creatures. Decorative scripts of this kind are found on bronzes dating from the Zhou dynasty (*c.*1050–221 BC) and on tiles of the Han dynasty (206 BC–AD 220).

The works Zhang has done in these scripts are characterized by lines painted in what is called 'flying white', a technique whereby a distinctive effect is produced when the brush is moved fairly rapidly across the paper and its drying hairs begin to separate. As they do so, they leave white lines within each brushstroke. The technique was first used by the famous calligrapher Cai Yong (133–192).

Zhang's own interpretation of 'flying white' is that the white represents the dreamlike or transient. The elegant curves and lines created by the 'flying' he regards as the most beautiful strokes in calligraphy. He feels that the combination of these two elements allows him to express sensations such as pleasure, insecurity, excitement, dreaminess (see fig. 56 on p. 63). Most of his pieces in 'flying white' have been done as soon as he wakes up in the morning, when he is still in a dreamy state of mind.

Just when Zhang had settled into enjoying his life as an artist in Beijing, his wife and two children announced that they wanted to live in Australia – not in a major city such as Sydney or Melbourne, but on the island of Tasmania. At first Zhang insisted that he could not leave China as it was the 'home' of calligraphy and the main source of his inspiration. However, he soon realized that while his art was already developing well, it might be good for him to get away from his traditional environment and absorb fresh ideas in new surroundings. When the family did set off for Tasmania Zhang was still in two minds about the move, but on arrival he was at once smitten by the island. Since 1992 he has lived part of the year there and part in Beijing.

The keen interest of the Australians in modern art and their receptiveness to Asian art in general have encouraged Zhang to experiment more boldly with his calligraphy. At the same time, the rugged landscape provides him with an endless source of inspiration. He finds the vast open spaces exhilarating and he is constantly fascinated by the peculiarities of the terrain. His time in Tasmania has served to remind him of the charm and strength of the abstract lines that are to be found in nature – an awareness that had lain dormant since his return to Beijing from China's virgin lands. In the vicinity of his home on the island he can observe the waves, the wind, striking cloudscapes, dramatic lines running through the rocks, and fine, delicate traces left on the beach by birds and animals. All have acted as stimuli for him to enrich and enliven his work.

Into another world

Even before moving to Tasmania, Zhang had felt that he would have to develop a more forceful calligraphic style if he was to convey his more intense feelings and depict some of the dramatic images that were surging through his mind. Once there, he began to experiment with denser ink, sometimes enriched with colour, and to use a fast-moving brush in order to create an impression of flight. He wanted to make his images so vivid as to seem to 'fly off the paper'. In 1994 he did a striking rendering of the Chinese character for 'dragon' (*long*). The force of this piece (fig. 133) relies not simply on the speed of the brush and the changing density of the ink, but also the way in which Zhang has reshaped the character to make it look like a dragon.

Towards the end of the 1990s Zhang was continuing to develop the ideas and techniques he had used in his 'flying white' script. His works had become progressively more abstract, and soon most of them were entirely

so. Collectively, he calls these pieces 'Dawo Black in White *Miaomo*', a description that Westerners have some difficulty in comprehending. Dawo, of course, is Zhang's given name, and the black and white refer to the colours of ink and paper respectively. When Chinese scholars talk about calligraphy and traditional painting, they use the word *momiao* to describe a particularly striking piece of work, *mo* referring to the ink and *miao* to the exceptional way in which it has been handled.

To describe his own work, Zhang turns this term on its head and makes it *miaomo*. He does this to make the point that he has created a new form of Oriental abstract expressionism. In it, he aims to reflect a spirit that is at once traditional and contemporary, Oriental and Western, and deeply reminiscent of both the natural and the man-made worlds. The trails of ink (the *mo* in *miaomo*) are intended to lead viewers to a portal through which they enter a world of total absorption in the wonders of art.

The forms of *miaomo* are abstract and without colour, but Chinese ink produces a wide spectrum of black tones and shades. Zhang executes his works in a single pass, with no secondary strokes or touching-up. His objective is to create art that is 'as natural as the wind blowing over water or the clouds gliding over mountains'.

Zhang's 1999 work *Black Moon* (*Xuan Yue*) encompasses many features of his characteristic style (fig. 134). The title comprises the contradictory elements of *xuan*, meaning 'black' or 'mysterious', and *yue*, the Chinese word for 'moon' or 'white'. In creating this large piece (135 × 350 cm)

134 Zhang thinks of his work *Black Moon* (1999) as a symphony without sound.

Zhang hoped not only to convey a sense of breaking free from conventional boundaries, by applying his ink in such a way that it appears to be flying off the paper, but also to overwhelm the viewer with the pleasures of abstract art through sheer scale. The idea for the piece stemmed from his belief that certain tones in music can induce such a powerful frisson of pleasure that what one hears does indeed seem to be 'the music of the heavenly spheres'. One of the ideas that Zhang intends to explore further is the interplay of the feelings induced by modern calligraphy and modern music.

In some of his other works Zhang seeks to highlight the links between traditional calligraphy and modern interpretations of it. In 1996 he produced a small volume entitled *Love Letters*. He began by taking a book of the beautiful writing paper produced at Rong Bao Zhai, the fine art shop in Beijing. In such books, printed on each page is a vertical rectangle outlined in red, with nicely proportioned margins around it. In traditional calligraphy, legible and meaningful Chinese characters are aligned in regular columns within these rectangular panels. Instead, Zhang not only painted bold, unrecognizable forms on the paper, in solid black ink, but allowed them to stray beyond the border of each panel. In doing so, he wanted to convey the message that love knows no bounds, but at the same time to imply that, to be worthy of love, the art of calligraphy itself needs to break free from the constraints of tradition.

In 2001 Zhang made this point even more dramatically in his *Letter* (fig. 135). The only words the piece contains translate as 'I've arrived!' – a slogan from Mao's Great Leap Forward campaign of 1958, which involved mobilizing the masses in the hope that China would quickly catch up with the developed world. More than forty years later, Zhang has used this old slogan in a new context. This time it celebrates the fact that China is stepping out into the world at the beginning of the new millennium, making a further 'leap' as it becomes ever more closely involved with the West, both culturally and commercially. Again the 'subtext' is that Chinese calligraphy and art, too, are at last being liberated from the confines of traditional thinking. As Zhang himself puts it, 'The peony is now stretching out beyond the garden fence.'

Zhang's fascination with both the drama and conversely the tranquillity that can be conveyed by the use of solid black in various forms has led him to produce a number of huge works, some as much as sixteen metres wide. Although large works are generally best viewed from afar, his pieces that are designed to induce tranquillity seem almost to embrace the spectator as he or she moves in closer. Whether in *miaomo* or solid black, Zhang's abstract works are unquestionably Chinese in feel. Their form, materials

234

135 Zhang's *Letter* (2001) proclaims 'I've arrived!', celebrating the greater extent to which China is venturing out into the wider world, and welcoming the Western world into China, at the start of the new millennium.

and texture leave no doubt as to their origins within Chinese calligraphy and Chinese culture. At the same time, however, their freshness and dynamism strike a chord with many Westerners.

Having already achieved three-dimensional effects on paper, Zhang's natural next step was to create truly three-dimensional calligraphic sculptures, which he began to do in 1996. In most of these works he emphasizes the line through the use of wire or strips of metal, but occasionally he creates more solid forms that are somewhat reminiscent of sculptures by Henry Moore.

Another of his departures has been into the genre of art photography. Wherever he goes, Zhang is quick to observe beauty of line and form, be it in a natural or a man-made context. His skill in capturing such beauty with a camera is demonstrated by an impressive collection of photographic images, which have been both exhibited and published.

More so than any other artist featured in this book, Zhang's love of nature is matched by his enthusiasm for modern technology. He uses digital scanners and printers to reproduce his work in albums, achieving such high definition that it would be easy to mistake the printed images for original works. While many of his calligraphic works are abstract, others still include readable – or just discernible – characters. His titles are often imaginative: one piece made up of the Chinese characters for clouds and rain carries the title *Sex between Heaven and Earth*.

Zhang's interest in technology extends to the Internet. He was the first of China's Avant-Garde calligraphers to have an e-mail address, and also the first to set up his own web site. Not only is his site well designed, but it has a first-rate English text, thanks to the language skills of his female companion.

When Zhang was in his forties and still living exclusively in China, he had already demonstrated that he was a highly imaginative and expressive artist whose calligraphy had such vitality that it seemed to 'fly off the paper'. More recently, since spending much of his time in Australia, he has pioneered his *miaomo* style of calligraphy as a medium through which both he and his audience can 'lose themselves' for a while – just as happens when one is wholly absorbed by music, food or sex. In doing so, he has played an important part in introducing the ideas of Western abstract expressionism into China.

PU LIEPING
1959–

Giving voice to abstract art

In his youth, Pu Lieping discovered that excelling at calligraphy not only won him praise from his fractious father, and his own peers, it also helped him to obtain good positions at work. In due course, however, his frustration with the rigid conventions of traditional calligraphy led him to develop an artistic style of his own. It goes well beyond the Modernist to place him firmly among the leaders of the Avant-Garde.

Good men have good calligraphy

When Pu was born in 1959, in Chengdu, the capital of Sichuan province, his parents were quite prosperous by the standards of the day. His father was the manager of a state-owned traditional Chinese medicine company and his mother worked as an accountant for the local government.

His home life changed radically when the Cultural Revolution got under way. In 1967, at the age of eight, he had the distressing experience of seeing his father harassed by the Red Guards and forced to wear a dunce's cap. By the time he emerged from detention a year later, Pu's father had changed. He was more authoritarian and aggressive than ever. Pu found this difficult to handle and soon became rebellious.

Although his parents were both quite good at calligraphy, as a child Pu refused to take an interest in the subject. Only in his early teens, when at his most impressionable, was he finally jolted into conforming with the Chinese tradition of acquiring good calligraphy skills in order to earn the respect of others. This came about because he was shocked to find himself the subject of three separate criticisms.

The first was made by a teacher, who, having seen a letter written by his mother, asked Pu why he could not write as well as she did. The second blow to his pride came when the illiterate peasants in his father's home village told Pu that they thought his calligraphy was awful, especially when compared with the fine Chinese New Year banners his father used to write out for them at his age. The ultimate indignity came when Pu's father made the comment, in front of him and his sister, that her calligraphy was much better than his.

Pu's response to these hurtful remarks was to begin studying calligraphy in secret. When his father began praising the improvement in his writing,

136 As he was entering his forties, Pu Lieping began experimenting with a new style of calligraphy which, although it drew on the symbols of China's heritage, was truly avant-garde.

he was delighted. For a while it seemed to soften his father's attitude towards him, but it was not long before the old frictions resurfaced and Pu's rebelliousness was rekindled.

In 1977 China's universities reopened after the Cultural Revolution. Pu applied to study natural sciences but failed to reach the required grade, having only recently switched to that subject from social sciences. However, because he was well liked by his teachers he was offered a junior post in Chengdu's newly established International Exchange Centre.

It proved an exciting place to work, as the Centre was soon tasked with handling an unprecedented range of educational and cultural exchanges. Pu was pleased to discover that his bosses respected him not just for his diligence as a cultural official, but for the quality of his calligraphy. This encouraged him to make even greater efforts to improve his skills. In 1980 he began taking private calligraphy lessons from Bai Yunshu, a leading local calligrapher and scholar. The following year, at the age of just twenty-two, Pu was rated among the ten best calligraphers in the province in an open competition. Commissions flowed in for him to produce name plaques for the new shops and hotels that were opening up in Chengdu in the wake of Deng Xiaoping's economic reforms. At last Pu's self-esteem was receiving the boost it had needed for so long.

In addition to teaching them the rules and techniques of calligraphy, Bai Yunshu made his students memorize and recite classical poetry. He hoped that through this practice they would absorb Daoist concepts of the harmony between man and nature and Buddhist teachings on life and death, and at the same time gain some insight into the broader currents of Chinese culture. Pu soon grew to appreciate that truly great calligraphy is rooted in a deep understanding of oneself, society and nature, and that it relies on the ability to express one's feelings on these subjects.

Grateful though he was for being helped to understand these key points, Pu was angry at Bai's refusal to teach him the more advanced forms of calligraphy until he had spent at least another decade improving his regular script. In 1983 he walked out of Bai's studio in a huff and determined to set about teaching himself. As his role models he chose two past calligraphers whose example he felt would help him find his own style. One was Mi Fu (1051–1107) and the other Huaisu (725–785), whose dramatic cursive script had so delighted Mao Zedong (pp. 105–17).

By 1986 Pu was beginning to feel that there was something fundamentally wrong with traditional calligraphy. He had now read many works on the theory of calligraphy, but it seemed to him that the authors were overly preoccupied with the minutiae of techniques, aesthetics and the links between personality and calligraphy. Not only did they seem to be writing about a craft, rather than an art, but it was one that was securely locked within the tight structure of Confucian society. Unlike Western art, which Pu had also been studying through the China Television University, Chinese calligraphy seemed to lack the rich corpus of works that provided a framework for the development of a creative art.

Breaking out

Pu so desperately wanted to create something entirely new that he began severing his contacts with traditional calligraphers. When Gu Gan's book *The Formation of Modern Calligraphy* appeared in 1986, he was overjoyed. Suddenly he was able to see a way forward. The Centre offered him promotion later that year, but he declined, preferring to stay in his present post because it gave him time to pursue his artistic interests.

Over the next few years he experimented along the lines proposed by Gu Gan in his book. The lessons Pu had been taking in traditional Chinese painting had given him a better understanding of composition and taught him how to place characters on the page in a more 'painterly' manner. The more he experimented within the framework of Modernism, however, the more he came to realize the extent to which the requirement to use only readable characters was imposing constraints on his own creativity. He wanted to find a way of employing calligraphic forms to express a sense of China's great heritage and to convey the essence of Chinese culture in a contemporary context.

In 1991 Pu started collecting together the works of sixty modern artists with a view to publishing them. In 1993 this material and a few pieces of his own appeared in his book *An Appreciation of Chinese Calligraphers' Works*. However, Pu was depressed by the outcome, which he felt amounted to an indictment of the state of modern calligraphy in China. It was clear that nearly all the pieces he had published were little more than variations on a theme already explored in the late 1980s. This only exacerbated his feeling that his own works lacked the depth for which he was striving.

The more Pu thought about this impasse, the more convinced he became that if Chinese calligraphy was to progress as a contemporary art form, then it needed to embrace a concept that would allow it to keep pace with all the changes taking place in society. He recognized that this was easier said than done, since even avant-garde artists in the West had difficulty in capturing the spirit of the modern world. But China was entirely different from the West, and he wanted it to spawn its own distinctive form of artistic expression.

Even in the early 1990s, Pu realized that China was going to be deeply influenced by its growing ties with other countries. The flow of information had brought about change in the past, but in the new technological age in which the country was becoming increasingly immersed, the influx of information was likely to have a far greater and more rapid impact.

The time had come, Pu believed, for Chinese artists to respond to Picasso's contention that calligraphy was, at least in part, an abstract art. He hoped also to see them trying out Western materials, colours, techniques and concepts. He was aware, however, that such experimentation would be a slow process, and that winning international recognition for Chinese calligraphy as a modern art could take even longer.

Visual music

Throughout the decade Pu experimented with what he called the creation of 'visual music'. Although he was still using readable characters, their shape and structure were now more distorted than a few years earlier. In one such piece he divided the paper into sixteen squares, arranged four by four, just as in the exercise books in which Chinese children practise their calligraphy. He then placed vaguely legible characters into each square, leaving the interplay between them and the white spaces that remained to create its own rhythms and tonalities.

His most important work in this series is *Autumn Wind* (fig. 137), which he did in 1995. It is inspired by one of Walt Whitman's poems, which Pu found so moving that he wanted to capture its 'music' in his calligraphy. He did so by modifying the Chinese characters into which the poem had been translated in such a way that their meaning was implied by their form. He then filled in the spaces between the characters with strokes of thin and thick ink to create a visual rhythm which he felt followed the cadences of the spoken words.

In 1998 Schubert's *Night and Dreams* became the direct musical inspiration for another of Pu's paintings. He had listened to the piece a number of times, and for him it conjured up images of a brightening dawn, rather than the darkness of night suggested by its title. In his own calligraphic interpretation of the music Pu included several oracle-bone characters, to emphasize the role they had played in the dawning of Chinese civilization. The title he gave his piece was *Music at Dawn*.

In 1999 he followed this up with another music-based work entitled *Pastoral Melodies* (fig. 33, p. 38). In this piece he wrote out the characters for 'ancestors', 'rain', 'fields', 'deer', 'ox' and 'bow' in oracle-bone script, which dates from the period Pu thinks of as the 'childhood of humanity'.

The characters are rendered not in the traditional black on white, but in white on brown. The white recalls bleached bones, while the brown background suggests the layers of sand and loess which over the centuries have buried the remains of ancient civilizations. The brown is burnished with gold to convey the value of the oracle-bone script, itself hidden for so long.

In explaining this work, Pu says that as we clear away the sands that have so long covered the traces of the past, we begin to hear the pastoral melodies of the childhood of humanity. The ancient Chinese characters he has used in it are intended to remind us of the heritage upon which the present is built.

137 In *Autumn Wind* (1995) Pu captures the bright autumn light of his home town, Chengdu, where that season is characterized by rich greens rather than golds.

A new structure

138 Pu's work *Dreams* (2000) is inspired by a line from Li Bai's poem *Night Feast*: 'This floating world is like a dream.'

Pu's real breakthrough into avant-garde art came in 2000, when he began to use calligraphic brushstrokes to underpin the structure of his compositions. He did this by writing out a few real characters on the paper with a wet brush, with one character usually overlapping one or more of the others. As the brushwork sinks into the paper, the result looks less like calligraphy and more like the kind of ink wash seen in Chinese painting. Even so, voids remain within the soft structure defined by his brushstrokes. The enchantment of such pieces owes a good deal to the lively texture of a

new type of Chinese *xuan* paper and the brightness of acrylic colours, in which Pu builds up his image over a base of traditional Chinese ink.

This new structural technique formed the basis for Pu's painting *Dreams* (fig. 138). Its composition and colours engender a feeling of the harmony of all things in a perfect world. On top of the basic structure he has drawn pictograms of tigers (a Chinese symbol of good fortune) that seem to be flying, and of birds and a deer. Rising out of the bluish landscape with its patches of warm autumnal colours are three-dimensional village houses, which evoke in many modern Chinese city-dwellers memories of a rural childhood. The 'dream' reminds others of Tibet, which in Chinese mythology was part of the realm of Heaven.

Pu uses the same structure in *The Future is Bright, but...* (fig. 139), also painted in 2000. In this work he vividly reflects the impact of the information age. The piece was inspired by the Chinese Government's plans to promote the development of western China, which includes Pu's home province of Sichuan with its 100 million inhabitants.

In *The Future is Bright, but...* the hoped-for influx of hi-tech industries into China is indicated by a star-shaped form suggestive of a space station. The pictogram in oracle-bone script of a bow and arrow symbolizes flight. Rows of pictograms of trees remind us of the need to protect the environment, while the small coloured patches (similar to those in Chinese folk paintings) focus attention on our need to preserve parts of our heritage from the encroachments of modernization. The character for 'survival' (*zai*) is included, along with a pictogram of a fallen banner, suggesting either earlier defeats or the risk of setbacks yet to come. Above all else, what catches the eye is the bright golden glow of the picture.

Over the past few years Pu has worked closely with other Modernist and Avant-Garde artists in China to breathe a new creative energy into the art of calligraphy. The Song Feng Xuan Gallery, which Pu and Wei Ligang (pp. 244–9) ran in Beijing from 1995 until 1998, provided a much-needed meeting place for members of the Avant Garde school and a venue for showing their works to a wider audience.

Pu's own major contribution to the promotion of Avant-Garde calligraphy has been the key role he played in organizing the 'Retrospective of Chinese Modern Calligraphy at the End of the Twentieth Century', staged in Chengdu in 1999, at which 400 works by more than fifty artists were exhibited. Without Pu's energy and enthusiasm, and the wide circle of contacts he has built up in Chengdu through working at the International Exchange Centre, it is doubtful whether this exhibition would ever have grown to such a scale.

139 In *The Future is Bright, but...* Pu expresses an optimism about the impact of economic development on China's western regions that is tempered by environmental concerns.

For several years Pu has been an untiring champion of the Avant-Garde school of calligraphic art in China. Above all, in his own work he has at last found his own form of expression, in which he uses abstract art to convey messages from China's cultural past, while at the same time voicing concerns about the future.

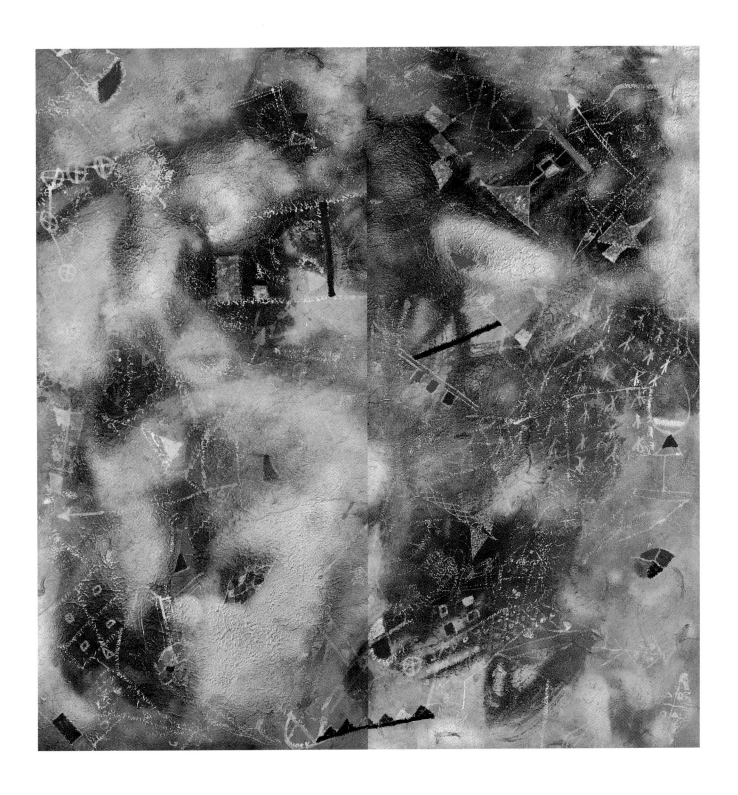

WEI LIGANG
1964–

The essence of calligraphy

Among China's modern calligraphers, Wei Ligang is not alone in being well versed in traditional styles and techniques. However, one way in which he is unique is that he comes from a scientific background. His familiarity with some of the arcane concepts of mathematics has no doubt informed his rigorous efforts to turn Avant-Garde calligraphy into a purely abstract art, albeit one that remains deeply rooted in Chinese culture.

From mathematics to art

Wei grew up in Datong, a major coal-mining centre on the railway line between Beijing and Mongolia. His father, who was the foreman of the city's vast railway marshalling yards, was a big, tough man who nevertheless had an artistic streak: he sang Chinese opera, performed as both a comedian and a magician, and carved charming wooden toys.

During the Cultural Revolution Wei's father was in charge of the wall in the railway yard on which posters were erected, some expressing the views of the workers, but the majority laying down the Party line. Wei was only eight when he wrote his first 'big-character poster', in chalk. A year or so later he started studying calligraphy in earnest. His father bought him some copybooks and his father's friends from the local propaganda department of the Party helped him with his technique. Before long he was able to write wall posters in good, clear script.

He also showed an early flair for creating cartoons. In 1975, when Deng Xiaoping was again being vilified, Wei got swept along by the political campaign. He captured the prevailing hostility of the Party line towards Deng so well in one of his cartoons that it was published in a local paper. Within a couple of years, however, Deng had been installed as China's new leader and Wei had become an admirer of his policies promoting economic reform and greater contact between China and other countries.

With the ending of the Cultural Revolution in 1976, schools were able to resume their teaching of traditional Chinese culture. This meant that the people of Datong could once more openly express their pride in the fact that their city had been the capital of the Northern Wei dynasty (386–535), during which period a thriving centre of Buddhism had been established at the nearby Yungang caves. The wonderful Buddhist sculptures and

140 Wei Ligang has developed a distinctive style of abstract calligraphy based on imaginary squares.

RIGHT: Detail of fig. 142

244

carvings that Wei saw there as a child sparked in him a life-long interest in Chinese culture.

At school he did so well in mathematics that in 1981, at the age of just seventeen, he was admitted to the prestigious Nankai University in Tianjin. Standards of calligraphy were high in the city as a whole, and the university itself had a flourishing calligraphy society that had been set up in the aftermath of the Cultural Revolution. Within two years Wei had become its president, which enabled him to meet all of the region's leading calligraphers. In particular, he spent much of his time with Li Henian, a scholar of long standing who knew all the main scripts and styles. He also got to know Wang Xuezhong, who taught calligraphy in Japan between 1981 and 1984 (when he was the first person to be sent from China for this purpose since 1949), and Sun Boxiang, whose mastery of the inscriptions of the Northern Wei dynasty was unrivalled and who was already experimenting with the reshaping of Chinese characters.

Wei felt that among all his contacts Wang Xuezhong was the one true artist. Even while he was serving as a vice-chairman of the Chinese Calligraphers' Association, Wang's own calligraphy was far from conventional. Wei was intrigued by the way he had introduced a new verve into his work by combining forcefulness, unpretentiousness and at times a touch of wildness within a novel calligraphic form. (Not surprisingly, Wang was one of the leading participants in the exhibition of Modernist calligraphy held in Beijing in 1985.)

Wei had already held a one-man exhibition of his calligraphy by the time he graduated in 1985. He had also decided to take up calligraphy full-time, but was not able to do so immediately because at that time the Chinese could still not choose their own occupations. The authorities assigned him to teach mathematics at the Teachers' Training School in Taiyuan, the capital of his home province. The museums in Taiyuan contain some fine archaeological treasures and are not far from Mount Tai, northern China's most sacred Buddhist mountain. In 1988, now aged twenty-four, Wei succeeded in persuading the school to let him teach calligraphy rather than mathematics.

From tradition to abstraction

It was in the same year that a book of his works was published under the title *A Collection of Wei Ligang's Calligraphy and Seal Cutting*. This demonstrated that Wei was not only a highly promising calligrapher and seal carver, but one who was already breaking free from the constraints of tradition. He was capable of producing a wide variety of works using different

245

ink and brush techniques. In some of these he supplemented his brushwork with penstrokes, which at that time was very novel. Several of his pieces were unquestionably Modernist in flavour.

One of the most innovative pieces illustrated in the book is based on a poem by Du Mu (803–852), *Drinking Fen Wine*. This work in particular reveals how Wei was already moving away from reproducing characters in their standard form towards writing them in a style that reflected the poetic sense of the phrase or poem they represented. To do this, he had set his characters against a fabric background that was grey, like the cloudy sky mentioned by Du Mu. He had then written out the individual characters with ink and brush in a modified form of oracle-bone script. Finally, he had traced them on to white paper, then cut them out and placed them on the cloth.

The overall effect was to make the characters resemble tears slowly trickling down a rough surface. Wei's style perfectly captures the maudlin mood of the poem, the only bright spot in the work being a red seal at the end, which looks rather like a small inn where people might be able to dispel their melancholy.

The 'Fen wine' of the poem takes its name from the Fen River, the main river in Shanxi province, on whose banks Wei was living at the time. He had named his studio the 'Place of Dancing in the Small Hut by the River' (his dancing partner being, of course, his brush). In 1994 he made a fascinating video of the work he was doing there. This provided further evidence that although well versed in traditional styles of painting and calligraphy, he was already exploring the abstract potentials of both arts. In the video he stresses his belief that the essence of calligraphy lies in the structure of the characters, not just the techniques of ink and brush.

As keen as he was to experiment, Wei still felt the need to master the techniques of the great calligraphers of the past. To help improve his wild cursive script, for example, he spent time practising the steady, balanced strokes of the regular script that Han calligraphers had inscribed on stone. He felt that this aided his control of the brush and thus enhanced the structure of his characters. He particularly liked using a medium-sized brush with very long hairs, which enabled him to produce a range of different ink effects with the same brush. This range was further extended by the way in which he sometimes scraped the hard shoulder of the brush, where the hairs are joined to the shaft, across the surface of the paper.

By the end of 1995 Wei had already had three one-man exhibitions in China. However, despite the popularity of his work, he was still dissatisfied with it. Even the prodigious amount of reading he had done on the theory

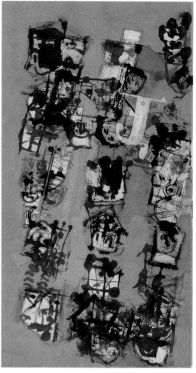

141 The slanting lines in *Wei's Square Frames J* create an impression of rain sheeting down. The raindrops are abstract 'characters' written in Wei's distinctive style. Contrasting with this very Chinese impression, the large white 'J' is intended to show that modern calligraphy can quite comfortably embrace elements of Western art and culture.

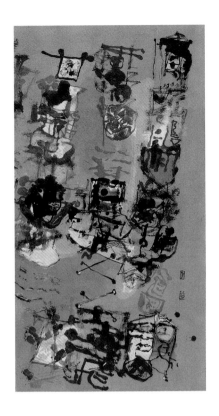

of calligraphy, both ancient and modern, seemed to offer him no way forward. To build on the direction his calligraphy had taken over the seven years he had been teaching the subject, he felt that he needed to make it more painterly – but that would require some new impetus or inspiration. It was at this juncture in his life that he accepted friends' advice and decided to go and live in the artists' village which then existed near the ruins of the Old Summer Palace on the northern outskirts of Beijing.

Moving there was a momentous step for Wei in that it would involve leaving his job and managing without a regular income. By now he was married with young twin daughters, so he would have to find ways in which his brush could earn him enough money to support the whole family.

With this in mind, he produced a series of abstract works in oil and acrylic on board. Some of them reflected his belief at the time that the lines one sees in nature are more elegant than any a calligrapher can create. The series proved tremendously popular. Wei showed several of the works at his 1995 exhibition with the intriguing title 'Worms, Itching Chinese Characters', which was held at the Song Feng Xuan Gallery that he had opened earlier that year in collaboration with Pu Lieping (pp. 236–43). It was China's first ever gallery to specialize in modern calligraphy.

'Wei's squares'

In 1997 Wei focused on the calligraphic aspects of his work in seeking to create a form of art that would have a wide appeal to contemporary taste, thus satisfying both his artistic ambitions and his need to attract buyers. In doing so, he explored two main themes. One centred on the range of modernistic effects that can be produced by employing traditional brush and ink techniques on Chinese paper. The other was based on what he calls 'Wei's squares' (fig. 141), a reference to his own modern interpretation of the notional square framework in which characters have always been rigidly positioned in formal Chinese calligraphy. These two themes characterize his work of the second half of the 1990s.

Wei has given some virtuoso performances with brush and ink, often incorporating several different techniques into a single work. Some parts of it may be rendered in deep, solid ink, while others consist of the merest traces from an almost dry brush. Most of Wei's compositions are devoid of any textual import, even when they do include a few barely readable characters, but the shape and texture of the linked brushstrokes often lead the viewer to imagine a fish, a bronze vessel or some other object.

When Chinese children learn calligraphy, the first thing they are taught is to place all their characters within square frames, in order to arrive at a balanced structure in which the text is neat and regular and the overall effect harmonious. Within each square are fine guidelines that determine the character's proportion and shape. Day after day, children practise writing characters within the squares printed on the pages of their exercise books. What Wei has done by basing his calligraphic art on these squares is to trigger an almost Pavlovian reaction in his Chinese audience. Whenever they see a square with lines in it, or lines that appear to be contained within an imaginary square frame, their eye automatically begins to search for a Chinese character.

Wei's piece *Wisteria Sinensis* (fig. 142) is inspired by an ancient Chinese poem on the beauty of Chinese wisteria. It consists of five lines of 'characters' in contrasting brushwork and densities of ink. By moving the brush slowly, he has created subtle effects of tone and line. The overall effect recalls wisteria cascading down in dappled sunlight. Even before starting on the piece, Wei had a clear idea of the composition he wished to create. As he wrote, he had real characters in his mind, which formed the basis of his abstractions. But soon after he had finished, he could no longer see the clues in the forms to remind him of the original characters.

Wei's aim in his calligraphy is not to provide textual gratification, but rather to compel the viewer to marvel at his artistic transformation of a

142 *Wisteria Sinensis* (2000) is a study in the subtle effects that can be created when the techniques of painting and calligraphy are combined.

142 *Wisteria Sinensis* (2000) is a study in the subtle effects that can be created when the techniques of painting and calligraphy are combined.

143 On the day he created this piece, Wei was feeling unwell but still had the urge to do some calligraphy. He found that as he wrote, the characters coming from his brush seemed to recall a poem by Ouyang Xiu (1007–72). The density of the ink in which the 'characters' are written ranges from the deep solid black of traditional calligraphy to shades of grey that are so pale as to be barely discernible. The strokes are knitted closely together, making the composition look like the arrangement of rafters in a typical Chinese roof.

tradition that stretches back more than 3,500 years. His abstract characters seem to exist as part of a mysterious personal visual language, while his works as a whole induce pleasure and excitement through their beauty, and fascination through their composition of lines, form and ink. For the Chinese, brought up to obey the unbending rules of traditional calligraphy, to gaze at Wei's art is like entering a floating world of dreams.

Wei's 'squares' come in many forms. In some of his works the squares descend in vertical lines, just as in traditional calligraphy (although his lines tend to be far less regularly perpendicular, sometimes even merging into each other). Occasionally he will write a classical poetic couplet in characters that are just readable, with the aid of an explanation from the artist. In other compositions the square frames do not descend in columns but look as if they are floating on the paper (fig. 143). This produces a dizzying effect similar to the impression one gets when watching the warriors in a Chinese opera, with their banners and wide costumes, twirling rapidly round and round on the stage.

Even Wei's totally abstract works convey a clear sense of being firmly rooted in Chinese culture. Although he constantly deconstructs and re-forms his characters, the influence of the original style of script still shows through in their basic shape, in the lines of their brushwork and in the densities of ink in which they are executed. Wei thus evokes echoes of the past by suggesting links with different periods in the history of Chinese calligraphy and with those calligraphers whose achievements have been most admired over the centuries.

He persists in his efforts to maintain a sharp distinction between calligraphy on the one hand and both Chinese painting and Western art on the other. He believes that abstract calligraphy, written on Chinese paper in Chinese inks, is not only a valid art form, but the only art form that is genuinely Chinese. If the Avant-Garde calligraphy of China is to be accessible to Westerners – which he is keen that it should be – Wei feels that it does not need to include explicit cultural content in the form of either discernible characters or clearly defined images. Its 'Chineseness' should be allowed to speak for itself.

WANG NANMING
1962–

Balls of criticism

Wang Nanming has been the most systematic of China's Avant-Garde calligraphers in terms of his efforts to make people think about the heavy burden imposed upon modern Chinese society by the country's culture and traditions. He does this not through 'shock art', but by continually repeating a single theme. He hopes that this repetition will, like the incessant dripping of water, have the power to erode even the hardest stone.

An independent outlook

Wang was brought up in Shanghai, the home town of both of his parents. His father worked as a government lawyer, and his mother, who came from a cultured family, as a teacher. Despite their relatively privileged background, Wang's parents did not suffer badly during the Cultural Revolution, largely because his father was a revered veteran of the war in Korea. Once the most violent phase of the Cultural Revolution had come to an end, in the early 1970s Wang's mother was able to pick up where she had left off and resume teaching him both Chinese painting and calligraphy – in very traditional ways.

Despite the fact that his independent way of thinking had made him something of a 'black sheep' at school, Wang reluctantly agreed to follow in his father's footsteps and enter the legal profession. From 1980 to 1983 he duly studied criminology at Shanghai's East China Law Academy. After graduating, he was assigned to the investigation bureau of the People's Procurators in Shanghai. Here he helped marshal evidence for use by the state prosecutors in court cases. In doing so, he learned much about the seamier side of life in the city that was the legacy of the Cultural Revolution and subsequent economic reforms.

Ever since childhood, Wang has loved calligraphy but hated all the rules surrounding the subject. As a teenager he found it wonderfully refreshing to attend lectures at which Professor Liu Zengfu (pp. 203–9) criticized the styles and techniques of some of the great masters. At the Law Academy he was lucky enough to have as his professor of classical Chinese Hong Peimo, a scholar in his forties who was already an exceptional calligrapher. It was Hong who first encouraged Wang to delve further into the styles of calligraphy that most interested him.

144 The spheres that dominate Wang Nanming's art are deeply symbolic and convey a strong message, which he hopes will change people's thinking.

Wang soon became intrigued by the strong calligraphy of Kang Youwei, the late nineteenth-century advocate of democratic reform in China. But he was influenced even more by Kang's recommendation that aspiring calligraphers should study the stone engravings carved by anonymous Wei craftsmen during the fifth and sixth centuries, rather than the polished brushwork of the Tang calligraphers of the seventh to tenth centuries.

Wang's passion for freedom of expression did not sit comfortably with his work of gathering evidence for the Procurators, whose task it was to enforce laws that allowed the individual few rights against the power of the state. In 1988 he took the brave step of giving up his job and setting out to become a freelance artist.

The late 1980s was a time of ferment in China. Both on the surface and beneath it, much was changing. While some people were becoming rich quite quickly, others felt cheated by the changes taking place, and by the all too visible signs of an upsurge in corruption. Although growing contact with the West had breathed new life into Chinese art, many of the young saw the ruling party and the government as continuations of the deeply conservative and authoritarian traditions of Chinese society and culture. It was in this climate that Wang began to develop his calligraphy.

He held his first one-man show, sponsored by the Communist Youth League, in 1988. In it he demonstrated his skill in the ancient styles of calligraphy that appear on bamboo strips dating back to the Han dynasty (206 BC–AD 220) and are found on stone inscriptions of the Northern Wei dynasty (386–535). The Party-sponsored newspaper *Youth Calligraphy* devoted two pages to lauding his achievements.

Despite the praise Wang's calligraphy had attracted, it did not bring him in enough money to make ends meet. Fortunately, this was not too serious a problem, as he soon found that he could earn a fair amount by writing about art and curating exhibitions. To begin with, however, a more ready source of income was teaching calligraphy to the children of Shanghai's newly prosperous businessmen.

While Wang was being commended for his skills as a traditional calligrapher, he was also making a name for himself as one of the pioneers of Avant-Garde calligraphy with his abstract 'Black Series' (fig. 145). At the Chinese Contemporary Calligraphy Exhibition held in Shanghai in 1991, he reinforced his reputation in this field by displaying works that broke the links with traditional calligraphy in a more radical way.

As visitors entered the exhibition they were confronted by a large sheet of calligraphy paper mounted on the wall, which looked like the book in which, on such occasions, visitors are invited to inscribe their names with

251

a brush. It bore the warning 'No signing with a brush'. Right at the outset Wang was trying to get across the point that the old habits were not acceptable and he wanted people to stop and think about the relationships between calligraphy, art and society.

Another of Wang's works on display nearby revealed his interest in deconstructing calligraphy. On top of a sheet of traditional calligraphy paper that he had laid out on the floor, he had arranged a number of black-painted fragments of the holed stones from Lake Tai that are more usually to be seen decorating Chinese gardens. Above them was the message 'New Action: Destroy Calligraphy.'

If he feels dissatisfied with a piece of work he has started on, Wang, like any other calligrapher, tends to scrunch the paper into a tight ball and throw it across his desk on to the floor. One day, when particularly displeased with his efforts, he noticed that there was something fascinating about the balls of rejected paper that were accumulating on the floor. Although the characters on them were not legible, the fragments of lines that could still be seen on the surface of the paper drew the eye directly to the beauty of the brushstrokes.

This discovery tied in neatly with his interest in deconstruction. Gu Gan (pp. 182–93) had already advocated taking characters apart so that their constituent elements could be displayed in a more painterly manner on paper. But Wang was more convinced by the argument of French philosopher and critic Jacques Derrida that conventional structures need to be broken down completely and recomposed.

Wang quickly came to see his discarded balls of paper as symbolic of the various contradictions surrounding calligraphy itself. In his view, as well as being an elegant traditional system of writing and the basis of an evocative form of modern art, calligraphy could be regarded as representing the darker side of Chinese society. He felt that over the centuries its purpose had been perverted in that it had been deployed as a mechanism for social control. Not only had the complexity of its scripts limited the spread of education and so blocked routes to privilege, but a cult of respect for calligraphic skills had been encouraged which ensured that the young deferred to their elders and the illiterate to the educated.

The Chinese had traditionally been taught from early childhood that their status in society would be defined by the quality of their calligraphy, and that achieving a high standard would require years of disciplined and repetitive copying of accepted styles. Only when their calligraphy teacher had decided that their work was good enough at one level would they be permitted to advance to the next. When people were finally deemed to have

145 Wang's *Black Series* of the late 1980s includes some of the most abstract modern calligraphy produced in China at that time.

mastered the techniques of calligraphy, they were allowed to develop their own style and to express themselves in their own way. By that time, however, their long years of submissive practice had usually made them too conservative to do anything other than continue to conform. The soft hairs of the brush thus proved more effective than an iron rod in making the young submit to the traditions of a hierarchical society, whether Confucian or Communist.

By screwing up a sheet of his work and throwing it away, an artist or writer clearly demonstrates his rejection of it. And in the Chinese language, as in English and others, the word 'balls' is a common expletive and a forceful statement of rejection. In the balls of paper that Wang now adopted as the hallmark of his art, he felt he had found the perfect graphic symbol for his rejection of the worst aspects of Chinese culture.

He was in no great hurry to show his new style of work. First, he wanted to mull over the ideas that underpinned it. It was not until 1992 that he felt ready to launch his sculptural calligraphy at an exhibition in Beijing, under the title *Combination: Balls of Characters* (fig. 146). The stir created by his exhibit was all the greater for the video that accompanied it, explaining how the balls had been made and the variety of ways in which they could be displayed.

Whilst in Beijing, Wang quietly took some strings of balls out to the Old Summer Palace. There he draped them over some of the stone fragments of the once grand baroque edifice, which had been designed for the emperor by the Jesuits in the eighteenth century. The point he was making was that the modernization of China requires far deeper change than the addition of Western decorative elements, be they economic, political or artistic.

Wang still likes to use strings of balls in his installations to convey an impression of tears of lamentation or falling raindrops that will slowly erode even the hardest stone. By the mid-1990s he was also piling up balls in ways which, at times, made them look like tombs in the Chinese countryside. He has since gone on to construct works in which the use of thousands of balls magnifies his theme of rejection.

Towards the end of the decade Wang began making his balls of calligraphy into objects in the shape of chairs, sofas, tables, stools, televisions and paintings hanging on a wall (fig. 147). Although the hundreds of balls from which each object is formed are all different, the overriding impression is that they are all made from the same material. This is Wang's way of protesting against what he sees as the banality of modern China's 'mass culture', which in his view is little more than a third-rate interpretation of old styles, devoid of modern creativity.

253

Promoting the Avant-Garde

For several years now, Wang Nanming has been actively promoting Avant-Garde calligraphy and art. He was probably the first person in China to act as an independent and professional planner for art exhibitions and workshops, a career he entered as early as 1994. Nobody knows the business of art financing in China better than he does, especially where contemporary works are concerned. Although Chinese companies are still far from enthusiastic about sponsoring contemporary art, Wang has been successful in building up a number of fruitful long-term relationships with overseas organizations.

Funding from the Arts Development Council in Hong Kong has enabled Wang to send one artist a month to work and exhibit there. Through a cultural funding committee of the German Government he has also been able to arrange for German artists to travel to China to meet and work with their Chinese counterparts. This has already enabled German artists to work in Beijing and the former German colony of Qingdao (1998), in Shijiazhuang (1999) and in Guangzhou (2000).

Wang has been active, too, as a writer and critic. Since 1992 he has been editor-in-chief of *Art Forum*, a contemporary art journal published

146 In her novel *Bath*, Yang Jiang said that calligraphic characters were the faces of the Chinese people. While the balls of calligraphy that make up Wang's three-dimensional piece do not reveal faces, they are packed closely together like a crowd silently making its statement.

147 By filling an entire room with furniture made from his balls of calligraphy, Wang was making his protest against the banality of mass production.

not in China, but in Taiwan. In 1994 he published *Understanding Modern Calligraphy*, his most important book to date, which was discussed at a symposium held on Mount Huang later in the same year. His other books include *Research on the History of Chinese Theories of Calligraphy* (1991), *The Interpretation of Modern Calligraphy* (1994) and *After the Conceptual – the Art and the Critic*.

Wang's works have been widely exhibited both at home and overseas. In addition to staging five solo exhibitions in China, he has participated in many others in China's three major cities: Beijing, Shanghai and Guangzhou. In Europe, his works featuring balls of calligraphy were first seen in Barcelona at the 1995 exhibition 'China: 15 Years of Vanguard Art'. The following year he had an installation exhibition at the Visual Arts Centre in Hong Kong. Thanks to his close links with the German art world (which have led to his acting as curator for two exhibitions at the German Embassy in Beijing), Wang's works were exhibited in Koblenz in 1999, Jena in 2000 and Mainz in 2001.

Wang's independence of mind has enabled him to develop a very personal style of art that makes a serious statement about life in China today. The balls that convey his message combine simplicity of form with depth of meaning, with the result that his works can be understood by Chinese and Westerners alike. Although he has constructed many objects from his balls of calligraphy, as yet none of these has been a bridge – but in many ways his work has indeed built a bridge between East and West. It has opened up a route by which foreigners are made to think more deeply about issues concerning modern-day China.

ZHANG QIANG

1962–

The creator of 'traceology'

148 As Zhang Qiang writes readable characters with his brush, his female partner moves the paper or object on which he is working, thus shattering, or deconstructing, his work. On the wall in this photograph are two of the 800 works he has created with the help of 100 different women.

Zhang Qiang is an artistic revolutionary with strongly conservative credentials. He has a deep understanding of traditional Chinese painting and calligraphy, and a thorough knowledge of the aesthetic theories that underpin them. He is also a leading theorist of the Avant-Garde movement in calligraphy and the founder of 'traceology', an entirely new genre that is centred on enlisting the aid of a female partner in creating each work.

The making of a theorist

Zhang Qiang was born and brought up in Shandong, the home province of both his parents' families. He describes his mother and father as 'revolutionary Communists'. In 1962, when he was born, his father was the head of a huge agricultural commune comprising some 30,000 people and his mother was in charge of its 'women's affairs'.

Ever since childhood, Zhang Qiang has been keen on art. At the age of thirteen he began to paint in a Western style. Although he was encouraged in this by his mother, his father was vociferously opposed to his 'wasting his talent in such an effete way'. So from an early age Zhang Qiang was locked in confrontation with his father. The rebelliousness this engendered in him was to spur his readiness to break free from artistic conventions.

On leaving school at seventeen, Zhang Qiang went on to the Taian Teachers' Training College, near Mount Tai, one of China's most famous scenic spots. Three years later, while teaching at the middle school in his home town of Feicheng, he began to take a serious interest in Chinese art. Since both painting and calligraphy were scholarly arts in China, he felt that he would only fully understand them if he first studied the theories on which they were based. Whilst doing so, he also spent time practising both traditional Chinese painting and calligraphy.

By 1985, at only twenty-three years of age, he had finished writing his first book, *Studies on Chinese Painting Aesthetics*. It was not published until 1993, but in the meantime he gained a certain notoriety within China's art world for his articles on Chinese art theory. This led to his being invited to take part in several national art conferences, at which he was invariably the most junior participant, in every sense. So stimulated was he by the lively debate at these events that he vowed to become a university professor.

Zhang Qiang moved a step closer to this goal when an exhibition of his paintings and calligraphy was staged in Jinan, the provincial capital, where he was invited to lecture at the Shandong Arts Institute. The Institute evidently did not share his father's view that 'the more he learns, the worse he becomes', because that same year it appointed him to its staff as a lecturer.

After the constant pressure of teaching at secondary-school level, Zhang Qiang was delighted by the relatively relaxed atmosphere of university life. He had little time to enjoy it, however, as he was soon assigned to teaching a course on the history of Western fine arts – a difficult subject, which his senior colleagues were keen to avoid. In order to prepare his lectures, Zhang Qiang had first to take a crash course in the subject himself. Although this was quite a challenge for him, the course was a great success. In 1993 the Institute appointed him director of the newly created Office of Fine Arts Studies, which was to supervise a new four-year degree programme on Western art history.

The same year Zhang Qiang published his book *A Comprehensive Review of Modern Calligraphy*. In it he rejected the idea espoused by the Modernists, led by Gu Gan (pp. 182–93), that calligraphy could be revitalized by restyling the characters and arranging them artistically rather than in the traditional straight columns or lines. The fact that foreigners were sometimes known to hang calligraphy the wrong way up by mistake reminded Zhang Qiang that one of Kandinsky's works was said to have been inspired by his seeing a painting hanging upside down in a Western art gallery. This, he felt, reinforced his own more radical argument that dispensing with the need to include meaningful text in calligraphy would provide much greater scope for developing it as a modern art form. At the same time, he recognized that persuading the Chinese to accept this suggestion could prove a lengthy 'psychological adventure'.

Three years later, in 1996, Zhang Qiang refined his theories further in his book *Broken Cubes in Games: Post-Modernism and Contemporary Chinese Calligraphy*. What troubled him most at this time was a feeling that calligraphy did not have a bright future. He pointed out that Western artists such as Pollock, Klee, Tapiès and de Kooning had all used the line as a form of abstract expression. Having seen the Miró exhibition in Beijing in 1995, he feared that modern Chinese calligraphy could end up as little more than a revival of early Western abstract art. A way out had to be found.

Traces of the brush

Zhang Qiang's fears for the future of calligraphy led him to reflect on its essential nature. In China the earliest pictograms are said to have been inspired by the footprints or traces of animals and birds. Zhang Qiang's starting point was that the whole history of Chinese culture could be seen as a series of traces: some strong, some faint, others invisible. If the art world accepted that all arts were traces of the culture that produced them, it could perhaps establish some common ground and escape from the endless debate over whether Avant-Garde calligraphy should be pigeonholed as either calligraphy or painting. This line of thought opened the way for Zhang Qiang to explore how the marks left on paper by brush and ink could be seen as the 'traces of the spirit'.

Zhang Qiang sought long and hard to put his own theories into practice by devising a new abstract style of calligraphy. Making little headway in his endeavours, he would resort to working when drunk or immediately after waking from a deep sleep. But even when he was in these 'altered states', his personality seemed stubbornly to persist in controlling his brush. Zhang Qiang's experiments not only proved debilitating, but did not have the desired effect of releasing the strong creative forces which he felt sure were within him.

It was in the aftermath of his divorce in 1993 that women entered the picture. Their presence was to spawn the creation of an innovative form of calligraphy which Zhang Qiang himself has dubbed 'traceology'. However, this was not a smooth process, nor did it lead quickly to success.

The first female partner whose aid Zhang Qiang enlisted in his experiments was a student of Chinese painting who wrote avant-garde poetry characterized by disjunctions of time and place. As she read her poems aloud, Zhang Qiang would try to write down the words in an abstract way. When he still failed to achieve the effect he was looking for, he began to think that he was getting too old to collaborate with such a 'trendy modern miss'. Nevertheless, the pair persisted with their experiments.

One night Zhang Qiang got the young woman to move his paper while he was writing down on it the words she was reciting. The results were better, but still did not constitute a breakthrough. Then a flash of inspiration made him turn his head away so that he could not see his partner while he was writing, although she could still see his hand moving the brush. This time the results amazed him. All of a sudden, he had succeeded in freeing himself from all the restrictions imposed by the conventional composition of characters. Over the next year or so he and the same partner produced another forty or fifty pieces in this manner.

In 1995 Zhang Qiang started working with other creative young women: first a calligraphy student, then a filmmaker, then a designer. He was soon struck by the fact that he was obtaining the best results from working with the filmmaker – the only one of his four partners who had no knowledge of either painting or calligraphy.

The more he conducted these experiments, the more Zhang Qiang felt that they should be carried out on a much broader scale. By working with a partner he had already created a distinctive form of calligraphy. By collaborating with a large number of partners he could create a whole artistic phenomenon. They must all be women, he insisted, since the difference between the sexes was a fundamental cultural and social divide and a powerful creative inspiration. In 1996 this led Zhang Qiang to embark on his five-year project 'Zhang Qiang's Report on the Study of Traces'. It was to involve cooperating individually with 100 different women.

The nature and scale of the project raised many a Chinese eyebrow. Some feminists accused Zhang Qiang of male chauvinism; after all, he did always explicitly take the lead, his brush could be seen as a phallic symbol, and his female partner was invariably relegated to the secondary role. Others voiced darker suspicions, despite Zhang Qiang's repeated assertion that he never entered into sexual relations with his artistic partners.

He prepared his Traceology Report (as it became generally known) very thoroughly. With each of the 100 women he created eight separate works, every one of them carefully documented. The woman would always decide on the type of brush, size of paper and amount of ink to be used. As she began to move the paper, Zhang Qiang would start writing sentences of real characters, in styles ranging from regular to cursive, according to his mood. The sentences he wrote out were usually fairly mundane thoughts that happened to be running through his mind, rather than the words of great Chinese poets or any of the poems he himself writes in classical style. The woman was never aware of what he was writing, and it was always she who decided when the session should finish.

Most of the volunteers who took part in the project found it an enjoyable, even a liberating, experience to be instrumental in the creation of Zhang Qiang's art. One of his assistants, a South Korean housewife, was so pleased with the outcome of their collaboration (figs 149 and 150) that she danced for joy. She claimed that the experience had evoked happy memories of her uninhibited childhood.

The 'traceology' collection is best viewed *en masse* (fig. 151). It then becomes clear that in some cases similarities exist within groups of works created with the help of the same woman. It is also interesting to note that when Zhang Qiang asked his partners which of their own eight pieces they liked the best, even those who knew nothing about art tended to choose the one he himself preferred.

Zhang Qiang has described and analysed the whole traceology project in a book entitled *Trace Aesthetics: Cultural Cross-overs through Art* (2002). In it he says that during the project he felt as if he was using his brush to construct a building while his partner was exerting an elemental force, like an earthquake, to destroy the whole structure. For him the shattered traces recall the moods of the women with whom he worked. Others, however, feel that they are like a Chinese version of the Rorschach ink-blot tests, with viewers projecting their own preoccupations on to what they see before them. One critic, Zhang Yiwu, sees Zhang Qiang's traces as representing universal issues such as the uncertainties of the post-Cold War era and concerns about sexuality and biotechnology.

Traceology in three dimensions

When Zhang Qiang was invited to take part in the exhibition 'Women's Art in the Twentieth Century' in 1998, he set about creating a different

149, 150 Zhang Qiang's partner in the creation of these two works was so pleased with them that she danced with delight.

form of traceology. Having already turned his calligraphy from a scholarly artistic pursuit into an exploration of the use of space in two dimensions, he wanted to experiment with more independent visual forms in three dimensions. He focused on the two most basic three-dimensional forms: the cube and the sphere. Zhang Qiang believes that these forms lie at the heart of Western art and so can act as a bridge linking East and West. To emphasize the point, he decided to work with only Western women on his new project. His installation works consist of long strips of paper on to which his female partner places plastic balls and cubes after he has painted them. Artist and assistant work on one section of the paper before unfolding the next. The woman decides whether she will lay the objects on the paper one by one as each becomes ready, or wait and position them all at once.

In addition to using plastic balls to suggest links between Eastern and Western art, Zhang Qiang also employs them in a purely Chinese context, aptly working with only Chinese female partners. For example, some of his works feature *taiji* balls bearing the symbols of yin and yang, which represent Daoism. In 1999 he used these at the 'Retrospective of Chinese Modern

Calligraphy at the End of the Twentieth Century' in Chengdu, in an installation he called the *Green City Mountain* after a local mountain famous for its Daoist temples. The Daoist belief in the essential harmony between man and nature has also inspired him to have his female partners throw their decorated white plastic balls into rivers, where they rotate as they float across the moving water.

Women are even more central to Zhang Qiang's art when their own bodies become the medium on which he paints. He has worked in this way with young Chinese women wearing black one-piece swimsuits, in order to create a harmony between their black costumes, their black hair and the ink he is applying to their exposed flesh. As before, the woman selects the brush that Zhang Qiang will use and decides how much ink he will have at his disposal. Turning away, he holds up his inked brush and starts writing, in the air, whatever thoughts are running through his mind. His partner, who can see the movement of the brush, brings her body into contact with it at will. Again, it is she who decides when the performance should stop.

Having been very pleased with the outcome of such work, Zhang Qiang would like to expand on the theme by creating a large outdoor installation in collaboration with 100 blonde women. Wearing white swimsuits and bearing the inkmarks he has painted on their bodies, the women will all gather and interact in the warm, shallow waters lapping a coastline of golden sand. If and when this dream ever materializes, its location is much more likely to be somewhere like Hawaii than any beach in China.

Zhang Qiang has already done a series of works featuring women in white. He has been collaborating since 1999 with a Beijing fashion designer specializing in Western styles, who makes dresses for him out of white calligraphy paper. These often elaborate creations are then put on by professional models, who assist Zhang Qiang in his art by allowing him to paint on the paper dresses they are wearing (fig. 152).

Another grand scheme Zhang Qiang has in mind is one that would require the cooperation of supermodels from the major Western fashion houses. Wearing white dresses that he had decorated with his brush, they would strut in turn down the catwalk in an impressive performance of abstract calligraphic art.

Although all art to some extent reflects the society in which it is created, Zhang Qiang does not consider his own work a direct manifestation of the changes that are currently taking place in China. He does, however, maintain that the very fact of his being permitted to perform and exhibit such innovative Avant-Garde art demonstrates how much attitudes in China have altered over the past decade.

Zhang Qiang has adopted a brave artistic approach to stimulating debate about perceptions of calligraphy and their cultural implications for Chinese society. One of his great strengths in doing so is that no one can accuse him of simply waving his brush about like an undisciplined child. He is a scholar and a professor, widely respected for his knowledge of the history and theory of both Chinese and Western art. His Avant-Garde calligraphic 'performances' are not only attractive and innovative, but carry a frisson of sexual excitement. Zhang Qiang is determined to explore his ideas further. Meanwhile, he is bracing himself for the day when a female artist reverses his concept and puts men in the submissive role.

YANG XIANYI

1915–

A collector of integrity

153 The collection that Yang Xianyi donated to the British Museum in 1995 is an excellent, and possibly unique, illustration of how calligraphy features in the private lives of individuals in modern-day China.

The turmoil caused by China's long and complicated political campaigns of the twentieth century led many people to betray those closest to them. For others, personal relationships became all the more intense as they faced the challenge with integrity, fortitude and loyalty to their friends. Yang Xianyi, one of China's leading literary figures and humanists, was at the centre of a circle of particularly close friends. Their calligraphy and inscribed paintings given to him and his English-born wife Gladys stand as a moving testament to the esteem and affection this couple have inspired.

English connections

Born the scion of a wealthy banking family, Yang soon showed signs of a precocious intellect. He was educated at the best English school in the British concession in Tianjin, and in 1934 went on to study Classics and English literature at Merton College, Oxford. Whilst there he indulged in pleasures high and low, writing poetry in several languages and gaining a reputation as something of a playboy. However, Yang was also extremely patriotic and took every opportunity to raise awareness of the suffering that Japan was inflicting on China.

His efforts in this direction were amply rewarded by an encounter with Gladys Tayler, a student of Chinese at Oxford who was helping with the anti-Japanese campaign. More than half a century later, Yang could still vividly recall the immediate impression made on him by this 'intellectual, athletic and dramatically good-looking young woman'.

In 1940 he and Gladys left Britain for China's wartime capital of Chongqing, where they were married. Within three years, Yang's exceptional command of English had led to his appointment as head of the government's Institute of Translation.

Following the defeat of Japan in 1945, Yang became so disillusioned by the corruption of Jiang Jieshi's regime that he started giving clandestine help to the Communists. Soon after the Communists won control of the country in 1949 the Yangs went to Beijing, where they were given leading positions with the Foreign Languages Press. Yang and Gladys worked together on translating Chinese literary classics into English and an extraordinary range of Greek and Latin literature into Chinese.

In Beijing they developed an impressive circle of friends from the literary and art worlds (many of whom feature prominently in this book). Among them were Huang Miaozi, the art historian who became a leading calligrapher, Wang Shixiang, famed scholar of so many of China's arts, the historian and calligrapher Qi Gong, stage-designer-turned-calligrapher Zhang Zhengyu, cartoonist Ding Cong, painter Huang Yongyu, and dozens of other literary scholars, writers and actors.

Although he had declined the honour of translating Chairman Mao Zedong's political and philosophical works into English, Yang remained one of those members of scientific and cultural circles in China who from time to time were invited to receptions to meet Mao and other leaders.

Yang never felt ill at ease at such events. On the first occasion, in 1954, Premier Zhou Enlai introduced him to Mao as the man who had translated into English the famous poem *Li Sao* by Qu Yuan (340–278 BC). When Mao expressed doubt that such a complex poem really could be translated, Yang replied, 'Chairman, surely all works of literature can be translated.' On another occasion, emboldened by a surfeit of alcohol at a banquet, Yang began making his way unsteadily to the top table to 'share a toast' with the Chairman. As he approached, the ever suave Premier Zhou Enlai leapt up, wine cup in hand, apologized to Yang that the Chairman no longer drank liquor, and offered to take a drink with him on Mao's behalf.

Because Gladys was classed as a 'foreign expert', the Yangs enjoyed a privileged lifestyle. But the good cheer that marked their life in Beijing in the early 1950s did not last long. While many of Yang's intellectual friends spoke out against the Communist Party during the 'Hundred Flowers Movement' of 1956–7, he himself did not. This was not through fear; he was still genuinely optimistic about the party leadership and the New China it had promised. However, the harshness of the punishments subsequently meted out to those who had been critical of the regime shocked him deeply and greatly diminished his admiration for Mao.

As the Cultural Revolution gathered momentum, Yang and Gladys felt increasingly threatened because of their foreign connections. Moreover, many of their literary translations had been of works now very much out of favour. The couple's fate was sealed when Mao's wife, Jiang Qing, called on the Red Guards to seek out foreign spies. A poem that Yang had written in support of Khrushchev's denunciation of Stalin quickly became instrumental in his own denunciation, replete with big-character posters, verbal abuse and a great deal of menace.

In May 1968 Yang and his wife were both sent to prison, but separately. Gladys was put into solitary confinement, since the authorities deemed

154 Wu Zuguang's toast to Yang Xianyi:

A hundred years is but a dream,
So let us get drunk and become immortal.

266

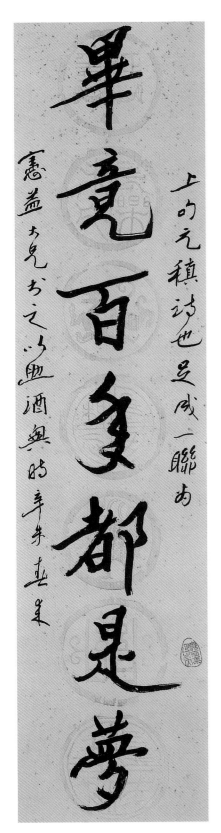

this more appropriate for a foreigner than being cooped up with ordinary Chinese 'criminals'. Yang's own spell in jail at least allowed him the comfort of the company of other prisoners, who between them had committed a wide variety of 'crimes'. Although his fellow inmates knew no English, to help while away the hours he taught them a song that had been popular in the days when he was studying in England, *Drink to me only with thine eyes*. He also taught them the famous Chinese poem *Song of Eternal Regret*, which is about the death of the Tang imperial concubine Yang Guifei.

In 1972, after four years in jail, both Yang and his wife were released and Yang was told that the case against him as a double agent had been 'cleared up'. The couple were allowed to return to their work on translating *A Dream of Red Mansions*, one of the great masterpieces of Chinese literature. Nevertheless, this remained a tense time, with the Gang of Four still very powerful.

Calligraphy and friendship

Soon other members of the Yangs' circle began to return to Beijing. In 1973 Wang Shixiang and his wife came back from the camps in the countryside where they had been detained for the previous few years. A couple of years later Yang's close friend and drinking companion Huang Miaozi was finally released after seven years in jail – the longest sentence imposed on any of his friends. However, the Yangs' joy at being reunited with their friends was overshadowed by the problems they were experiencing with their son. The conflicting loyalties with which he had had to cope both during and in the wake of the Cultural Revolution had left him confused and unwell. In 1975 he was taken to England, where it was hoped he would recuperate. Instead, on Christmas Day he committed suicide.

After the suffering the Yangs and their friends had all endured, the bond between them assumed an even greater significance. Members of the circle would frequently confirm and celebrate their friendship by presenting each other with gifts of pieces of their calligraphy. These varied widely in quality, but whether the text written out was a newly composed poem or a carefully chosen extract from a classical work, it always conveyed the spirit of true comradeship.

On 2 April 1976, at the time of the Qing Ming festival when the Chinese traditionally sweep the graves of their ancestors, huge crowds gathered in Tiananmen Square to pay homage to the late Premier Zhou Enlai. When he had died that January, the Gang of Four had thwarted all attempts at public mourning, thus intensifying the mass outpouring of sentiment that was to be seen on the occasion of this traditional event.

155 Fan Guan's erudite condemnation of the Gang of Four, here written out in the hand of Pan Jijiong, is replete with commentary and includes information on one of the Gang's henchmen from the records of the Shanghai Police Department.

The following evening the painter Lin Kai and his wife called to see the Yangs. After they had all had a lot to drink and become rather maudlin, Lin Kai's wife, who had a hauntingly beautiful voice, began singing a well-known song of which the first stanza praised Mao, the second Zhu De (Mao's great military commander) and the third Zhou Enlai. As soon as she got to the third stanza, everyone broke down in tears. Lin Kai later marked the moment with a poem lamenting that there would never be another man of Zhou Enlai's stature to guide China (fig. 156). The future looked bleak.

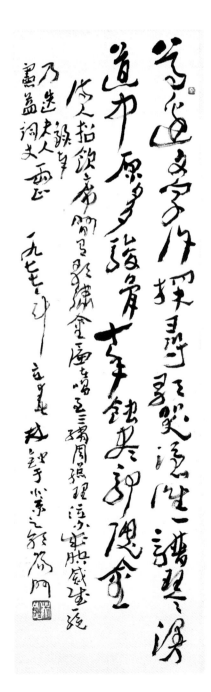

156 Lin Kai's poem lamenting the death of Premier Zhou Enlai expressed the feelings of most Chinese in the period immediately following his death.

Some people have money to buy fine horses.

For the past ten years, however, the gold has rusted and no horses have come.

There are, in fact, no longer such horses.

Even before the overthrow of the Gang of Four in October 1976, Yang and his friends Huang Miaozi, Pan Jijiong and Lu Jian were secretly exchanging poems expressing their hatred of them and everything they represented. Despite the layers of classical erudition that masked the true meaning of these verses, each piece of calligraphy would be prudently destroyed as soon as it had been circulated and read. However, each writer committed his own poems to memory.

Once the Gang of Four were safely in jail, Yang and his friends carefully rewrote some of their poems and gave them to each other to keep. The British Museum now has a small collection of these pieces of calligraphy. In one, Huang Miaozi calls, in his own words, for the overthrow of the Gang of Four (see p. 175). In the hand of poet-calligrapher Lu Jian is the moving poem *Red Leaves of the Western Hills*, composed by Marshal Chen Yi in the autumn of 1966. In another piece, Pan Jijiong, formerly a journalist with the pro-Communist Hong Kong newspaper *Wen Wei Po*, has written out a scathing poem by Fan Guan on the activities of the Gang of Four (fig. 155).

However, not all the calligraphy that Yang received from his friends and colleagues was political in content. Wu Sichang, one of the leading authorities on *A Dream of Red Mansions*, presented him with a sad piece about his own life. Wu's poem expresses his regret at having spent his middle years overseas (he returned home from England in 1962) and so missed out on the excitement of the creation of New China. Now that he has been back in China for fifteen years, he feels old. He was not the best of scholars in his youth, nor has he achieved very much in later life. He wonders who will mourn him after his death.

Other friends gave Yang pieces that were more celebratory in mood. In 1974 the artist Huang Yongyu had exhibited a painting of two owls, one of which had one eye closed. With some justification, Jiang Qing and her supporters had taken this as an affront to Chinese Communism and vilified him for it. Huang was therefore greatly cheered when he heard of the fall of the Gang of Four. He was happier still when a related item of news reached him in the spring of 1977, which prompted him to add the following note to another owl painting that he gave to the Yangs (fig. 157):

Since ancient times some people have liked owls and some have not. I just painted owls because they seemed interesting. But that woman Wang reported to Jiang Qing that it was an inauspicious bird and therefore the meaning of my painting was suspect. Well, now I hear that Wang has committed suicide – perhaps in her case the owl was inauspicious.

269

157 This painting by Huang Yongyu celebrates the end of the Cultural Revolution.

The years of reform

By early 1979 the tensions within China had eased considerably. Deng Xiaoping had secured control of the Party and set the country on the road to economic reform. He had also begun to address the ill-treatment inflicted on so many people during the Cultural Revolution. It was a good time for Yang Xianyi and his circle, who celebrated the new relaxed atmosphere with a great deal of socializing and drinking. The dramatist Wu Zuguang and Huang Miaozi both gave Yang pieces of calligraphy on the theme of drinking and friendship (fig. 154).

Yang and his painter friend Huang Yongyu were greatly amused by the sudden upsurge in enthusiasm for calligraphy after the Cultural Revolution. This prompted Huang to do a new painting (fig. 158), to which he appended the message:

We don't know which calligrapher this old man is, because there are now so many – just like bamboo shoots after the rain – that it is difficult to remember all their names.

158 In 1979 Huang Yongyu
gently mocked the sudden upsurge
in the Chinese people's enthusiasm
for calligraphy.

Yang soon became China's best-known literary emissary. Over the next few years he travelled to Australia, Japan, India, Hong Kong and also several European countries, including the United Kingdom. During a visit to Ireland in 1981 he brought tears to the eyes of his hosts with a spirited rendering of *Danny Boy*. Three years later he was able to return to Oxford to spend a term at Merton College, where he had studied in the 1930s.

Yang now felt that China was on the right political course. The country needed gradual progress, not further upheaval. He supported Deng Xiaoping's decision in 1983 to clamp down on those who had been putting up posters on 'Democracy Wall', calling for greater freedom. Then in 1985, for the first time in his life, he decided to join the Communist Party. The same year, as part of Deng's efforts to make amends for the excesses of the Cultural Revolution, along with many other intellectuals Yang was appointed a member of the Chinese People's Political Consultative Conference (CPPCC).

But events in Tiananmen Square in the spring of 1989 were to unsettle his political outlook yet again. As the crowds of demonstrators gathering in the square grew bigger and bigger, Yang became increasingly angered by the antagonistic attitude of the leadership. He began adding his name to the petitions destined for the CPPCC and other official organizations, which pleaded with the government to listen to the voice of the people, implement political reforms and permit some freedom of the press.

Not long after the suppression of the demonstrations, Yang was quietly expelled from the Party and no longer received official invitations to travel

overseas. He was touched and cheered when his old friend Wang Shixiang presented him with a pair of scrolls (fig. 159) on which he had written:

Since ancient times, all saints and scholars have been lonely.
Those famous for their literary talents, however,
are known for being romantics.

Now that he was more than seventy-five years old and no longer burdened by official responsibilities or the need to work at translations, Yang began to devote more time to writing the finely crafted poems that he refers to as his 'doggerel'. Although still firmly in favour of many of the economic and social changes that were taking place in China, he despised the rise in corruption and the decline in moral values.

In 1996 a volume of poems by Yang, Huang Miaozi and Shao Yanxiang was published. Its content was predominantly satirical or political, but not to the extent of provoking the displeasure of the authorities. The cartoon portrait of the group that appears at the front of the book illustrates the mood of their works very well. All three are dressed in traditional scholarly garb, but with markedly unscholarly smiles on their faces, and each carries his best-known attribute. For Huang this is a calligrapher's brush, for Shao writing paper... and for Yang a bottle of scotch and some glasses.

Further evidence of the high regard in which Yang is held as a poet was provided when the Chinese newspaper *Zheng Xie Bao*, published by the CPPCC, invited him to write a poem to commemorate Britain's handover of Hong Kong to the Chinese on 30 June 1997. If the editor was expecting some rousing nationalistic poem, he must have been sorely disappointed. But if what he wanted was a more subtle view of events for his intellectual readership, then he could not have done better:

Losing sovereignty and territory – it was a shameful thing.

I still remember how the flag of surrender was hoisted
over the walls of Nanking.

To peddle for drugs and send a fleet, it was not a just war.
But to close up frontiers and lock up the empire,
it was not normal behaviour either.

The desolate spot today has become a trading post.
A useless islet has now turned into a treasure trove.

We celebrate together the return of the pearl
and friendship is enhanced.

272

Meeting with a smile – all hostility and gratitude forgotten.

159 Wang Shixiang's pair of scrolls in tribute to his good friend, Yang Xianyi.

The words were finely balanced. On the one hand, Yang's verse refers to the unjust seizure of the territory. On the other, it recognizes that, under the British, Hong Kong became a 'treasure trove'. His final line is a gem of poetic and political insight.

The poem appeared on the front page of the *Zheng Xie Bao*. It sat alongside a large full-colour photograph of the celebratory fireworks cascading over the bright lights of Victoria and Hong Kong harbour. Underneath was another photograph – of Yang, smiling enigmatically and with a glass of scotch in his hand. It was at Oxford that he first developed a taste for whisky, a drink that was to afford him some comfort throughout many difficult years. It is appropriate that he chose a glass of it to celebrate this historic event.

After a long illness, Yang's wife, Gladys, died in the year 2000. When friends asked him which of all the passages they had translated together over the years now came to mind, he recited the following lines from a poem that forms part of *A Dream of Red Mansions*:

Now you are dead, I come to bury you.
  None has divined the day when I shall die.
Men laugh at my folly in burying fallen flowers;
  but who will bury me when dead I lie?
See, when spring draws to a close and flowers fall,
  this is the season when beauty must ebb and fade.
The day that spring takes wing and beauty fades,
  who will care for the fallen blossom or dead maid?

It was a hauntingly beautiful tribute to the closeness and fondness that had made Yang Xianyi and Gladys Tayler the perfect translating team.

ILLUSTRATION AND PHOTOGRAPHIC CREDITS

Photographs of all British Museum works © The British Museum, provided by courtesy of the Department of Photography and Imaging.

FULL-PAGE ILLUSTRATIONS

p. 2   Han Yu, detail of fig. 121
p. 6   Zhang Dawo, *Letter*, 2001 (see fig. 135)
p. 8   Huang Miaozi, *Mit Diesen Händen*, 1990, courtesy of the artist
p. 10   Zhang Zhengyu, detail of fig. 21
p. 14   Huang Miaozi, detail of fig. 103
p. 40   Sa Benjie, detail of fig. 131
p. 66   Deng Sanmu, detail of fig. 75
p. 118   Li Luogong, detail of fig. 86
p. 132   Qi Gong, detail of fig. 94
p. 162   Wang Dongling, detail of fig. 101
p. 194   Zhang Sen, detail of fig. 113
p. 226   Wei Ligang, detail of fig. 142
p. 264   Zhang Zhengyu, detail of fig. 83

NUMBERED FIGURES

1   Classical calligraphy, detail of fig. 97
2   Modern calligraphy, detail of fig. 25
3   Neo-Classical calligraphy, detail of fig. 120
4   Avant-Garde calligraphy, detail of fig. 142
5   Seven scripts, courtesy of Huang Miaozi
6   Wang Xizhi, anonymous copy, detail of *Clearing after Snowfall*, National Palace Museum, Taipei, Taiwan, Republic of China
7   Yan Zhengqing, detail of a rubbing of *The Daoist Priest Qingyuan's Poetry*, private collection
8   Huaisu, detail of *Autobiography*, National Palace Museum, Taipei, Taiwan, Republic of China
9   Mi Fu, detail of *Poem written in a Boat on the Wu River*, The Metropolitan Museum of Art, New York
10   Zhao Mengfu, detail of *The Origin and Transmission of the Preface to the Orchid Pavilion*, National Palace Museum, Taipei, Taiwan, Republic of China
11   Dong Qichang, detail of *Poem of the Immortal Lu*, National Palace Museum, Taipei, Taiwan, Republic of China
12   Calligraphy practice, private collection
13   The Four Treasures of the Scholar's Studio, The British Museum
14   Chinese brushes, courtesy of Gu Gan
15   Chinese dots and lines, courtesy of Gu Gan
16   Wang Shixiang, *Requiem*, courtesy of the artist
17   Shen Yinmo and Liu Zengfu, courtesy of Liu Zengfu
18, 19   Shen Yinmo, two details of his calligraphy, private collection
20   Qi Gong, detail of fig. 94
21   Zhang Zhengyu, Sun Ran's poem on the Da Guan Lou at Kunming, courtesy of Huang Miaozi
22   Gu Gan, *World of Supreme Bliss*, 1991, 121 × 123 cm, OA 1996.6-14.027, Add. 661, gift of the artist
23   Mountains, courtesy of Gu Gan

24   Clouds, courtesy of Gu Gan
25   Orchids, courtesy of Gu Gan
26, 27   Constructing *Jue Wu* ('Realization'), courtesy of Sa Benjie
28, 29, 30   Ink effects, courtesy of Gu Gan
31   Zhang Sen, *Watching the Clouds*, 1999, 92.3 × 44.4 cm, OA 2002.1-30.021, Add. 755, gift of Gordon and Kristen Barrass
32   Sa Benjie, *From Confusion to Clear-mindedness*, 1995, each scroll 131.5 × 21.5 cm, OA 2002.1-30.019, Add. 753, gift of Gordon and Kristen Barrass
33   Pu Lieping, *Pastoral Melodies*, 2000, 65 × 65 cm, OA 2002.1-30.023, Add. 731, gift of Gordon and Kristen Barrass
34   Wu Shanzhuang, *Red Room*, courtesy of Wu Shanzhuang and Ethan Cohen Fine Arts, New York
35   Nanjing Road, Shanghai (1936), private collection
36   Children writing calligraphy, poster, private collection
37   Shen Yinmo writing New Year scrolls, courtesy of Chu Jiaji
38   Sha Menghai's name plaque for the Da Xiong Bao Dian Pavilion, Hangzhou, private collection
39   The Hundred Flowers Movement, private collection
40   Writing big-character posters, poster, private collection
41   Mao Zedong's *Mount Liupan*, Shanghai Airport, private collection
42   Mao Zedong's *Bombard the Headquarters*, poster, private collection
43   Writing Cultural Revolutionary Posters, poster, private collection
44   Li Luogong and his rendering of Mao's poem beginning 'I lost my proud poplar', courtesy of Ding Bokuei
45   Tiananmen Square, Beijing, April 1976, private collection
46   Huang Miaozi, *The Will of the People*, 1977, each scroll 118.3 × 29.3 cm, OA 1996.6-14.04 (a,b), Add. 638, gift of Yang Xianyi
47   Picasso and Zhang Ding (1956), courtesy of Zhang Ding
48   Gu Gan, *Overturning the Mountains*, 1985, 93.5 × 87.5 cm, OA 1996.6-14.025, Add. 659, gift of the artist
49   Bai Qianshen, unreadable characters, courtesy of the artist
50   Wang Dongling, *View from Heaven*, 1987, courtesy of the artist
51   Xu Bing, *A Book from the Sky*, installation at the Elvehjem Museum of Art, University of Wisconsin-Madison, 1991, courtesy of the Elvehjem Museum of Art
52   Jiang Zemin, *Shen Zhou*, 2000
53   Qi Gong writing a company logo, private collection
54   Gu Gan's *Heart to Heart* on the label of Château Mouton Rothschild, 1996, courtesy of the artist
55   Wang Nanming, *Balls* installation, courtesy of the author
56   Zhang Dawo, *Flying White*, c.1995, 67.3 × 56.6 cm, OA 1998.2-10.04, gift of the artist
57   Geng Biao with calligraphy, 1995, private collection
58   Children's calligraphy class, Hangzhou, 2000, private collection

59   Shen Yinmo, courtesy of Chu Jiaji

60, 61   Shen Yinmo, *Homage to Wang Xizhi*, 1955,
29.4 × 58.5 cm, OA 2002.1-30.01, Add. 735,
gift of Gordon and Kristen Barrass

62   Ye Gongchuo, courtesy of Huang Miaozi

63   Ye Gongchuo, *Country Elegy*, late 1950s, 150 × 38.8 cm,
OA 2002.1-30.02, Add. 736, gift of Gordon and Kristen
Barrass

64   Guo Moruo, courtesy of Guo Pingying

65   Guo Moruo, detail of *Manjianghong*, 1964, courtesy of
Guo Pingying

66   Guo Moruo, *Mount Wu Yi*, 1962, 69.5 × 43 cm, private
collection, on loan to The British Museum

67   Guo Moruo, *The Ancient Pine*, 1960s, 83 × 170 cm,
OA 2002.1-30.03, Add. 737, gift of Gordon and Kristen
Barrass

68   Guo Moruo, *Smash the Gang of Four*, 1976, 51 × 56.5 cm,
OA 2002.1-30.04, Add. 738, gift of Gordon and Kristen
Barrass

69   Marshal Chen Yi, courtesy of Chen Haosu

70   Chen Yi, *Mount Morgan*, 1952, courtesy of Chen Haosu

71   Chen Yi, *Qingdao*, 1954, courtesy of Chen Haosu

72   Chen Yi, *Chengdu*, 1955, courtesy of Chen Haosu

73   Chen Yi, *Kunming*, 1961, courtesy of Chen Haosu

74   Deng Sanmu, private collection

75   Deng Sanmu, *The best have been rounded up*, 1958, each
scroll 138 × 21.3 cm, OA 2002.1-30.05 (a, b), Add. 739,
gift of Gordon and Kristen Barrass

76   Mao Zedong, private collection

77   Mao Zedong, *Huichang*, 1935, 50 × 30 cm, private
collection, on loan to The British Museum

78   Mao Zedong, *Red Flag*, 1958, courtesy of the British Library

79   Mao Zedong, *The Long March*, 1962, enlarged facsimile,
36 × 145 cm, OA 2002.1-30.024, gift of Gordon and
Kristen Barrass

80   Mao Zedong, *Swimming*, 1956, enlarged facsimile,
88 × 170 cm, OA 2002.1-30.025, gift of Gordon and
Kristen Barrass

81   Mao Zedong, detail of *The Indomitable Soul*, 1962, private
collection

82   Zhang Zhengyu, courtesy of Huang Miaozi

83   Zhang Zhengyu, *Premonition*, 1966, each scroll
136.8 × 33.8 cm, OA 1996.6-14.020 (1-2), Add. 654,
gift of Yang Xianyi

84   Zhang Zhengyu, *Ode to a Plum Blossom*, early 1970s,
92.7 × 173 cm, OA 2000.6-12.01, Add. 733

85   Li Luogong, courtesy of Ding Bokuei

86   Li Luogong, *The Indomitable Soul*, 1981, 32 × 179.5 cm,
OA 2000.11-28.01, Add. 719, gift of Gu Gan

87   Li Luogong, *Eternally Youthful Art*, late 1970s,
83.5 × 47 cm, OA 2002.1-30.06, Add. 740, gift of
Gordon and Kristen Barrass

88   Sha Menghai, courtesy of Wang Dongling

89   Sha Menghai, *Hangzhou in Spring*, 1980s, 67 × 52 cm,
OA 2002.1-30.07, Add. 741, gift of Gordon and Kristen
Barrass

90   Lin Sanzhi, courtesy of Wang Dongling

91   Lin Sanzhi, *Going up the Hill*, 1975, 135 × 34 cm,

OA 2001.2-14.02, Add. 729

92   Lin Sanzhi, *Buddhism and Books*, 1988, 133.2 × 31.2 cm,
OA 2002.1-30.08 (a, b), Add. 742, gift of Gordon and
Kristen Barrass

93   Qi Gong and Gordon Barrass, private collection

94   Qi Gong, *The Differences between Beijing and Guangzhou*,
1984, each scroll 127.5 × 31.5 cm, OA 2001.1-14.01
(a, b), Add. 728

95   Wang Shixiang and his wife, courtesy of the artist

96   Wang Shixiang, *Don't Laugh at Me*, 1996, 53 × 69 cm,
OA 2002.1-30.09, Add. 743, gift of Gordon and Kristen
Barrass

97   Wang Shixiang, *Returning*, 1994, 65.5 × 45 cm,
OA 1996.6-14.030, Add. 664, gift of the artist

98   Wang Dongling, courtesy of the artist

99   Wang Dongling, *Tiger*, 1986, 66.8 × 67 cm,
OA 1988.5-16.01, Add. 518

100   Wang Dongling, *Feeling and Passion*, 1999, 56 × 81.2 cm,
OA 2001.5-24.01, Add. 730, gift of Michael Goedhuis

101   Wang Dongling, *The Void*, 2000, 272 × 142.5 cm,
OA 2001.2-3.01, Add. 722, gift of the artist

102   Huang Miaozi, courtesy of the artist

103   Huang Miaozi, *Maintaining Standards*, 1995, each scroll
138 × 34 cm, OA 2002.1-30.013, Add. 747, gift of
Gordon and Kristen Barrass

104   Huang Miaozi, *Great Changes*, 1993, 68.5 × 64 cm,
OA 2002.1-30.010, Add. 744, gift of Gordon and Kristen
Barrass

105   Huang Miaozi, *Clouds*, 1992, 65 × 31.5 cm,
OA 2002.1-30.11, Add. 745, gift of Gordon and Kristen
Barrass

106   Huang Miaozi, *The Gentleman Scholar*, 1994, 69 × 44 cm,
OA 2002.1-30.012, Add. 746, gift of Gordon and Kristen
Barrass

107   Huang Miaozi, *The Night Feast*, 1996, each scroll
155 × 61.1 cm, OA 2002.1-30.014, Add. 748,
gift of Gordon and Kristen Barrass

108   Gu Gan, courtesy of the artist

109   Gu Gan, *Walking Alone*, 1994, 50 × 51 cm,
OA 1996.6-14.028, Add. 662, gift of the artist

110   Gu Gan, *Opening Up*, 1995, 99 × 101 cm,
OA 1996.6-14.029, Add. 663, gift of the artist

111   Gu Gan, *The Age of Red and Gold*, 2000, 95.2 × 120.5 cm,
OA 2000.11-28.02, Add. 720, gift of the artist

112   Zhang Sen, courtesy of the artist

113   Zhang Sen, *Ferrying South to Lizhou*, 1994, each scroll
183 × 49.5 cm, OA 1996.6-14.03 (a–d), Add. 637,
gift of the artist

114   Zhang Sen, *The Lantern Festival*, 1994, 131.4 × 66.8 cm,
OA 1996.6-14.01, Add. 635, gift of the artist

115   Liu Zengfu and his daughter, private collection

116   Liu Zengfu, *Finding your Place*, 1996, each scroll
178 × 48 cm, OA 1996.6-14.024 (a, b), Add. 658,
gift of the artist

117   Liu Zengfu, *The Vast Expanse of China*, 2000, courtesy of
the artist

118   Liu Zengfu, *Graceful Rhythms*, 1995, 136 × 51 cm,
OA 1996.6-14.023, Add. 657, gift of the artist

119 Han Yu, courtesy of the artist

120 Han Yu, *Falling Leaves*, 1993, each scroll 131 × 33 cm, OA 2002.1-30.015, Add. 749, gift of Gordon and Kristen Barrass

121 Han Yu, *Seeing Things in Perspective*, 1996, each scroll 131 × 34.5 cm, OA 2002.1-30.016, Add. 750, gift of Gordon and Kristen Barrass

122 Sa Benjie, courtesy of the artist

123–8 Sa Benjie, *The Furniture Family*, 1994, each 34 × 47 cm, OA 2002.1-30.017 (a–f), Add. 751, gift of Gordon and Kristen Barrass

129 Sa Benjie, *Fable about a Table*, 1994, 31.7 × 41.3 cm, private collection

130 Sa Benjie, *Let Yourself Go*, 1997, 53 × 37.8 cm, OA 2002.1-30.018, Add. 752, gift of Gordon and Kristen Barrass

131 Sa Benjie, *Realization*, 2000, 68.5 × 68.5 cm, OA 2002.1-30.020, Add. 754 , gift of Gordon and Kristen Barrass

132 Zhang Dawo, courtesy of the artist

133 Zhang Dawo, *Dragon*, 1995, 37.2 × 45 cm, OA 1998.2-10.02, Add. 686, gift of the artist

134 Zhang Dawo, *Black Moon*, 1999, 135 × 350 cm, courtesy of the artist

135 Zhang Dawo, *Letter*, 2001, 179.3 × 97 cm, OA 2001.10-12.01, Add. 734, gift of the artist

136 Pu Lieping, courtesy of the artist

137 Pu Lieping, *Autumn Wind*, 1995, courtesy of the artist

138 Pu Lieping, *Dreams*, 2000, courtesy of the artist

139 Pu Lieping, *The Future is Bright, but...*, 2000, each scroll 134 × 66 cm, OA 2001.2-3.02, Add. 723, gift of the artist

140 Wei Ligang, courtesy of the artist

141 Wei Ligang, *Square Frames J*, 2000, courtesy of the artist

142 Wei Ligang, *Wisteria Sinensis*, 2000, 68.2 × 135 cm, OA 2001.2-3.03, Add. 724, gift of the artist

143 Wei Ligang, *Homage to Ouyang Xiu*, 2000, courtesy of the artist

144 Wang Nanming, courtesy of the artist

145 Wang Nanming, Black Series, 1990, each scroll 69 cm square, (left) OA 2001.10-3.01, Add. 732, gift of the artist, (right) courtesy of the artist

146 Wang Nanming, *Balls*, installation, late 1990s, courtesy of the artist

147 Wang Nanming, *Balls Furniture*, 2000, courtesy of the artist

148 Zhang Qiang, courtesy of the artist

149 Zhang Qiang, *Traceology*, late 1990s, 88.5 × 64 cm, OA 2001.1-30.01, Add. 721, gift of the artist

150 Zhang Qiang, *Traceology*, late 1990s, 88.5 × 64 cm, OA 2002.1-30.022, Add. 721, gift of Gordon and Kristen Barrass

151 Zhang Qiang, *Installation*, 1999, courtesy of the artist

152 Zhang Qiang, *Painted Lady*, 2000, courtesy of the artist

153 Yang Xianyi, courtesy of the artist

154 Wu Zuguang, *Drunken Immortality*, 1979, each scroll 127.2 × 30 cm, OA 1996.6-14.014(a,b), Add. 648, gift of Yang Xianyi

155 Pan Jijiong, *Down with the Gang of Four*, 1977, 54.8 × 34.4 cm, OA 1996.6-14.015, Add. 649, gift of Yang Xianyi

156 Lin Kai, *Lamenting the Death of Zhou Enlai*, 1976, 113.1 × 33.5 cm, OA 1996.6-14.018, Add. 652, gift of Yang Xianyi

157 Huang Yongyu, *Auspicious and Inauspicious Owls*, 1977, 48 × 45.5 cm, OA 1996.6-14.012, Add. 646, gift of Yang Xianyi

158 Huang Yongyu, *Old Calligraphers*, 1979, 57.8 × 45 cm, OA 1996.6-14.019, Add. 653, gift of Yang Xianyi

159 Wang Shixiang, *Homage to Yang Xianyi*, 1990, courtesy of Yang Xianyi

CHINESE TRANSCRIPTIONS OF CALLIGRAPHY

The English translations given on pp. 170–1 and on pp. 115, 116, 117 and 129 have been adapted, respectively, from those published in D.C. Lau, *Translation of the Tao te ching*, London: Penguin, 1963, and Xu Yuanzhong, *Song of the Immortals: An Anthology of Classical Chinese Poetry*, Beijing: New World Press, 1994, after comparison with the original Chinese.

Listed by figure number in order of appearance.

page 這雙手

10　你曾洗過一百萬遍
而且總是干淨純潔清白
沒有人害怕將它握住
雖然你曾用它
把致人死命的榴彈
向發生器的炮口裝填
德國海因利希·伯爾遺
作《用這雙手》的幾句。
一九九一年郝大錚譯，
苗子以商周文字書之。

21　昆明大觀樓對聯（孫髯翁撰）五
百里滇池，奔來眼底，披襟岸
幀喜茫茫空闊無邊。看東驤神
駿，西翥靈儀，北走蜿蜒，南
翔縞素。高人韻士，何妨選勝
登臨。趁蟹嶼螺州，梳裹就風
鬟霧鬢。更萍天葦地，點綴些
翠羽丹霞。莫孤負四圍香稻，
萬頃晴沙，九夏芙蓉，三春楊
柳。
數千年往事，注到心頭，把酒
凌虛嘆滾滾英雄誰在。想漢習
樓船，唐標鐵柱，宋揮玉斧，
元跨革囊。偉烈豐功，費盡移
山心力。盡珠簾畫棟，卷不及
暮雨朝雲。便斷碣殘碑，都付
與蒼煙落照。只贏得幾杵疏鐘
，半江漁火，兩行秋雁，一枕
清霜。

22　極樂世界

31　行到水窮處，坐看雲起
時。王摩詰詩句。張森

32　一塌糊涂，才識凹凸。

44　蝶戀花：答李淑一
我失驕楊君失柳，
楊柳輕揚直上重霄九。
問訊吳剛何所有，
吳剛捧出桂花酒。
寂寞嫦娥舒廣袖，
萬里長空且為忠魂舞。
忽報人間曾伏虎，
淚飛頓作傾盆雨。

46　十萬狂花如夢寐，
九州生氣恃風雷。

48　山摧：
地崩山摧壯士死，
然後天梯石棧相鉤連。

50　泰山成砥礪，
黃河為裳帶。

52　神州

54　心

57　鳥語花香

60　九月十七日羲之報旦因孔侍中
61　信書想必至不欲領軍慶後問憂
懸能須申忘心故肯遣取消息羲
之報得示知足下猶未佳耿耿吾
亦劣明出乃行不欲觸霧故也遲
散王羲之頓首
一千九百五十五年六月廿日遣
興臨此　　　　　　尹默

63　幾處弄歌繞翠微，
一天細雨濕羨衣。
春山得意渾無事，
白鶴遠從煙杪歸。
花草栽培萬棘刪，
谷山村落有餘閑。
莽鶩飛鳥原無定，
恰共晴雲出岫還。
蔣青先生雅屬。葉恭綽

66　關上松林密，
閩江一覽中，
人來摷石鼓，
我欲撫蒼空，
千嶺波濤涌，
群帆煙雨蒙，
車隨山路轉，
如看萬花筒。

67　六朝遺植尚幢幢，
一品大夫應屬松。
吐出虯龍思后土，
松直鸞鳳訴蒼空。
四山有石泉聲抱，
萬里無云日照融。
化作甘霖灌九域，
千秋長愿割年豐。
東山下有普照寺，寺內有松一
株，云系六朝時物。枝幹渾然
龍虬來俯垂致　地。

68　水調歌頭：粉碎四人幫
大快人心事，
揪出四人幫。
政治流浪，文痞，
狗頭軍師張。
還有精生白骨，
自比則天武后，
鐵帚一掃光。
篡黨奪權者，
一枕夢黃粱。
野心大，
陰謀毒，
詭計狂。
真是罪該萬死，
迫害紅太陽。
接班人是俊杰，
遺志繼承果斷，
功績何輝煌。
擁護華主席，
擁護黨中央！
一九七六年十月二十一日作於
北京。郭沫若

73　昆明新年
1961年1月2日

忽報歲除俱歡然，
滿堂鼓掌迎新年。
建設鬥志更奮發，
不畏長征有困難。

座上總理傳電訊，
北京歡慶同昆明。
大家遙祝主席好，
保證今年取豐盈。

晚會已散不能散，
臨散同志更依依。
再話今年新形勢，
戰販已到日落西。

元旦游湖驚浩淼，
扁舟千仞望龍門。
青青麥秀遍原野，
錦繡河山畫不能。

紅旗隊隊走不停，
二日機場送遠行。
中緬友好添新頁，
祥雲朵朵護機群。

75　鴻雁又南飛，
　　驚嘆歲月如流，
　　海角天涯終來相憶 。

　　鱸蓴新有味，
　　盡入漁樵罟綫，
　　臨詩載酒還與誰同。

77　清平樂：會昌
　　東方欲曉，
　　莫道君行早。
　　踏遍青山人未老，
　　風景這邊獨好。
　　會昌城外高峰，
　　顛連直接東溟。
　　戰士指看南粵，
　　更加鬱鬱蔥蔥。

79　長征
　　紅軍不怕遠征難，
　　萬水千山只等閑。
　　五嶺逶迤騰細浪，
　　烏蒙磅礴走泥丸。
　　金沙水拍雲崖暖，
　　大渡橋橫鐵索寒。
　　更喜岷山千里雪，
　　三軍過後盡開顏。

80　水調歌頭：游泳
　　才飲長沙水，
　　又食武昌魚。
　　萬里長江橫渡，
　　極目楚天舒。
　　不管風吹浪打，
　　勝似閑庭信步，
　　今日得寬餘。
　　子在川上曰：
　　逝者如斯夫！
　　風檣動，
　　龜蛇靜，
　　起宏圖。
　　一橋飛架南北，
　　天塹變通途。
　　更立西江石壁，
　　截斷巫山雲雨，
　　高峽出平湖。
　　神女應無恙，
　　當驚世界殊。

81　老驥伏櫪，志在千里。
　　烈士暮年，壯心不已。

83　望崝嶸而勿迫，
　　恐鵜鴂之先鳴。

84　風雨送春歸，
　　飛雪迎春到。
　　已是懸崖百丈冰，
　　尤有花枝俏。

俏也不爭春，
只把春來報。
待到山花爛熳時，
她在叢中笑。

86　神龜雖壽，
　　猶有竟時。
　　騰蛇乘霧，
　　終為土灰。
　　老驥伏櫪，
　　志在千裏；
　　烈士暮年，
　　壯心不已。
　　盈縮之期，
　　不但在天；
　　養怡之福，
　　可得永年。
　　曹操詩龜雖壽

87　歲月留不住，　書畫葆青春。
　　高莽同志囑正，駱公。

89　紅杏墻頭粉蝶，
　　綠楊窗外黃鶯。
　　何處春風最好？
　　蹋青人在蘇堤。

91　遠上寒山石徑斜，
　　白雲生處有人家。
　　停車坐愛楓林晚，
　　霜葉紅于二月花。

92　影從月地參禪佛
　　日據書城作寓公

94　瓊島暮霞孤塔迥
　　珠江明月畫船秋

96　阿旋愛吃長茭白，
　　歪角偏耽匍地青。
　　草味薰猶心漸識，
　　牽來無不惬牛情。

　　日斜歸牧且從容，
　　緩步長堤任好風。
　　我學村童君莫笑，
　　倒騎牛背剝蓮蓬。

　　架竹栽籬覆草茅，
　　為牛生犢築新牢。
　　但求母健兒頑碩，
　　慰我殷勤數日勞。

　　初生犢子方三日，
　　已解奔騰放四蹄。
　　他日何當挽犁耙，
　　湖田耕遍向陽堤。
　　咸寧雜詩丙子冬暢安

97　美酒葡萄白氈陳
　　殷勤相勸意情真
　　言歸先計重來日
　　西出陽關有故人

99　虎

100　感

101　無

103　行己有恥，博學於文

104　氣象萬千

105　帶雨雲埋一半山

106　鴉柿訛成雅士圖
　　饞涎貪吻笑縱哺。
　　何當下海摸金去，
　　飽殘終朝大丈夫。
　　雅士圖。苗子

107　夫天地者萬物之逆旅，
　　光陰者百歲之過客。浮生
　　若夢，為歡幾何。古人秉
　　燭夜游良有以也。

109　古路無行客，寒山獨見君。

110　開一古國之門

111　紅金時代

113　澹然空水對斜輝
　　曲島蒼茫接翠微
　　波上馬嘶看棹去
　　柳邊人歇待船歸
　　數叢沙草群鷗散
　　萬頃江田一鷺飛
　　誰解乘舟尋范蠡
　　五湖煙水獨忘機
　　溫庭筠七律
　　[利州南渡]

114　東風夜放花千樹
　　更吹落，星如雨
　　寶馬雕車香滿路
　　鳳簫聲動，玉壺光轉
　　一夜魚龍舞
　　蛾兒雪柳黃金縷
　　笑語盈盈暗香去
　　眾裏尋他千百度
　　驀然回首，那人卻在
　　燈火闌珊處
　　稼軒[辛棄疾]青玉案，元夕

116 虎氣必騰上
　　河漢湛虛明

117 大漠孤煙直
　　長河落日圓

118 自作新詞韻最嬌
　　小紅低唱我吹簫
　　曲終過盡松陵路
　　回首煙波十四橋

120 西風渭水
　　落葉長安

121 就日瞻雲
　　目極八荒

123 三好叔子圖。老借畫
124 老子英雄兒好漢圖騰。老借
125 嚇！瞧這一家子
126 椅上有人五百多春。
　　物存，人說話亦存，人不存。
127 金婚小照
128 半夜醒來，一切都靜悄悄
　　的，別的甚麼都沒有只有
　　一片空白。有時會突然思
　　如泉湧，想起很多稀奇古
　　怪，好象從來沒有這麼敏
　　捷，也沒有這麼聰明過。
　　坐上此椅一定會有同感，
　　嗚呼坐禪！甲戌夏暑熱，
　　寫此納涼。

129 有這麼一張畫案，甚麼人用過
　　它不知道，有甚麼畫是在它上
　　邊畫的也不知道，更不知是甚
　　麼人多事搞來的木頭，甚麼人
　　出了式樣，甚麼人用鏃鑿斧鋸
　　把它做成了這般模樣，只知道
　　它被人賣了。買家也并不愛它
　　也并不把它當回事兒，而是要
　　把它拆了做成其它甚麼東西再
　　賺錢。案子傷心地哭了。真沒
　　想到活了這一把年紀下場這麼
　　慘。也許是命不該如此，有個
　　好心人爲它贖了乃收留了它。
　　這面案子事大不一樣了。被新
　　主人重新這麼一倒，新主人親
　　自拉着車，案子坐在車上，可
　　神氣呢。案子被送到了火車站
　　，平生第一回坐上了火車。到
　　了它的新家，主人特別珍愛它
　　。它也很愛這個新家。案子好
　　，有了新家，有了知音，而興
　　奮不已。高興着時間就過得快

有很多天沒見到它的男主人了
。案子有點納悶，又聽說外邊
出了甚麼事兒，案子真替它的
主人揪心。果不出所料，案子
後來聽別人說它的知音被打成
了右派，而且罪名之一就是因
爲它。案子從來沒有過過這麼
傻(窩)囊的事兒，覺得太對不起
朋友了。是它連累了救命恩人
，不應該啊！可桌子一丁點辦
法也沒有。後來一群吵吵鬧鬧
的人把它載了去，非要讓它揭
發批判它的恩人。桌子一聲不
吭，那些人沒轍了。幸虧當時
它已不值甚麼錢，那些人還留
着它，一口氣盼着有那麼一天
它還會交得出甚麼新問題來。
桌子被押到地下室，一擱就是
十年。不知怎的桌子又神奇地
回到家裏，見到了它日日夜夜
想的主人。男主人更是珍愛有
加。後而由細心地女主人在上
面寫寫畫畫。不知不覺被他們
夫婦編入了他們的一本著作。
桌子出名了，知道它的人越來
越多。主人心裏雖然舍不得，
但又不得不替桌子想，給它找
一個最好最好的歸宿。桌子也
舍不得患難的知己，也舍不得
這個家。再後來主人心一橫找
了一座香火挺盛的廟把桌子擱
了。

130 鬆了自由，放了自在。

131 覺悟

133 龍

134 玄月

135 信：我來了！

154 畢竟百事都是夢
　　何如一醉便成仙

155 百怪魚龍雜
　　都乘歇浦濤
　　元戎打砸搶
　　干將剪摸掏
　　(注)如陳阿六者偷兒上海市公安
　　局三次逮捕有案
　　管蔡能讒旦
　　師昭欲代曹
　　鐵拳砰一擊

小丑甬安逃
輕搖羽毛扇
緊貼石榴裙
(注)
貪眼窺黃閣
兇心撰黑文
當年攻魯迅
三月剿田軍
天網疏無漏
薰蕕畢竟分
鏡殿連鍾室
妖姬穢史傳
篡權斜老眼
獻舞賣芳年
念念清君側
聲聲近日邊
安劉留至計
華岳聳中天
元良驚溘逝
鬼蜮禁哀思
鹿馬超前古
忠奸混一時
倉皇水滸傳
快意震災詩
女帝黃粱夢
喇叭鳴咽吹
方管討四害詩書請憲益先生教
正。潘際坰丙辰冬於北京。

156 萬遍文字何探尋，
　　歌哭口口一譜琴
　　漠道中原多駿骨，
　　十年蝕盡郭槐金。

157 鴟梟之爲物有史以來皆纏夾於
　　毀吉之間。餘對此鳥年來頗有
　　興趣，嘗信手寫之。實無意以
　　狀物言事，謬牝王某云此鳥不
　　祥，乃君主立名目罪以深刻含
　　義娘子野心。矛頭所指不言自
　　明。聞王某已自動作古。不祥
　　云云頓成自我寫照。造化弄人
　　奇詭若是。噫嗟。憲益兄一笑
　　。黃永玉補記。

158 此老古人然不知何位書家。天
　　下書家雨後春筍，正勞好記性
　　也。

159 從古聖賢皆寂寞
　　是真名士自風流

279

BIBLIOGRAPHY

Calligraphy and calligraphers

Bai Qianshen, 'From Wu Dacheng to Mao Zedong: The Transformation of Chinese Calligraphy in the Twentieth Century', in Maxwell K. Hearn and Judith G. Smith (eds), *Chinese Art: Modern Expressionism*, New York: Metropolitan Museum of Art, 2001.

Billeter, Jean-François, *The Chinese Art of Writing*, Geneva: Skira, 1990.

Chang, Leon L.-Y. and Peter Miller, *Four Thousand Years of Chinese Calligraphy*, Chicago: University of Chicago Press, 1990.

Chiang Yee, *Chinese Calligraphy: An Introduction to its Aesthetic and Technique*, London: Methuen, 1938.

Clunas, Craig, 'Wang Shixiang', *Apollo*, November 1987.

Ellsworth, Robert Hatfield, *Later Chinese Paintings and Calligraphy, 1800–1950*, 3 vols, New York: Random House, 1987.

Farrer, Anne, *The Brush Dances and the Ink Sings: Chinese Painting and Calligraphy from the British Museum* (exh. cat.), London: Hayward Gallery, 1990.

Farrer, Anne (ed.), *Twentieth-century Painting and Calligraphy at the British Museum*, London: Saffron Books, forthcoming.

Fong Wen, *Beyond Representation: Chinese Painting and Calligraphy, 8th–14th Century*, New York: Metropolitan Museum of Art, 1992.

Fu Shen C. Y., *Traces of the Brush: Studies in Chinese Calligraphy*, New Haven: Yale University Art Gallery, 1977.

Gu Gan, *The Three Steps of Modern Calligraphy*, Beijing: China Books Publishing House, 1990.

Gu Gan, *The Art of Gu Gan*, Beijing: China Cultural Relations Press, 2000.

Gu Wenda, *The Mythos of Lost Dynasties, 1984–1997*, Hong Kong: Hanart TZ Gallery, 1997.

Harris, Robert E. Jr and Wen C. Fong, *The Embodied Image: Chinese Calligraphy from the John B. Elliot Collection* (exh. cat.), Princeton, NJ: Princeton University Art Museum, 1990.

Hearn, Maxwell K, and Judith G. Smith, *Chinese Art: Modern Expressionism*, New York: Metropolitan Museum of Art, 2001.

Holcombe, Charles, *In the Shadow of the Han: Literati Thought and Society at the Beginning of the Southern Dynasties*, Honolulu: University of Hawaii Press, 1994.

Hu Shiping, *Wang Shixiang: The Beachcomber of Gems in Chinese Relics*.

Hwa, Khoo Seow and Nancy L. Penrose, *Behind the Brushstrokes – Appreciating Chinese Calligraphy*, Hong Kong: Asia 2000, 1993.

Kwo Da-Wei, *Chinese Brushwork in Calligraphy and Painting: Its History, Aesthetics and Techniques*, New York: Dover Publications, 1990.

Ledderose, Lothar, *Mi Fu and the Classical Tradition of Chinese Calligraphy*, Princeton, NJ: Princeton University Press, 1979.

Ledderose, Lothar, 'Chinese Calligraphy: Its Aesthetic Dimension and Social Function', *Orientations*, XVI, October 1986.

Lindqvist, Cecilia, *Empire of the Written Symbol*, London: HarperCollins, 1991.

Schlombs, Adèle, *Mit diesen Händen: moderne chinesische Malerei und Kalligraphie der Kunstler Gu Gan und Huang Miaozi – Eine Ausstellung des Museums für Ostasiatische Kunst* (exh. cat.), Cologne: Museen der Stadt Köln, 1992.

Song Zhongyuan (ed.), *The Art Works of Wang Dongling*, Hangzhou: Chinese Academy of Fine Arts Press, 1994.

Sullivan, Michael, *The Three Perfections: Chinese Painting, Poetry and Calligraphy*, New York: George Braziller Publishers, 1980 (revised edition published 1999).

Sullivan, Michael, *Arts and Artists of Twentieth-Century China*, Berkeley: University of California Press, 1996.

Tseng Yuho, *A History of Chinese Calligraphy*, Hong Kong: Chinese University Press, 1993.

Wang Fangyu, *Dancing Ink: Pictorial Calligraphy and Calligraphic Painting*, Hong Kong, 1984.

Wang Nanming et al., *Dialog Fernost*, Jena: Jenaer Kunstverein e. Verlag, 2000.

Wang Shixiang, *The Charms of the Gourd*, Hong Kong: Next Publication, 1993.

Wang Tao, 'Tradition and Anti-tradition in Contemporary Chinese Calligraphy', in Anne Farrer (ed.), *Twentieth-century Painting and Calligraphy at the British Museum*, London: Saffron Books, forthcoming.

Watt, J. C. Y. and C-t Li (eds), *The Chinese Scholar's Studio: Artistic Life in the Late Ming Period* (exh. cat.), New York: The Asia Society Galleries, 1987.

Yang Yingshi, 'New Trends in Chinese Calligraphy, 1898–1998', www.asiawind.com (Honolulu 1998).

Yang Yingshi, 'The Creation of Modern Calligraphy in the Context of Contemporary International Culture', in *Bashu Parade: '99 Chengdu Retrospective of Chinese Modern Calligraphy at the End of the Twentieth Century* (exh. cat.), Chengdu: Sichuan International Cultural Exchange Center, 1999.

Yang Yingshi, 'A Chronology of Chinese Modern Calligraphy', www.china-gallery.com/en (Beijing, 2000).

Zhang Yiguo, *Brushed Voices: Calligraphy in Contemporary China*, New York: Columbia University Press, 1998.

Zhu Qingsheng, *The International Conference on Words and Writing*, December 2000, Taiwan Museum of Art (ISBN 957 02 7374 7).

History

Baum, Richard, *Burying Mao*, Princeton, NJ: Princeton University Press, 1994.

Garside, Roger, *Coming Alive! China after Mao*, London: Andre Deutsch, 1981.

Goldman, Merle, *Sowing the Seeds of Democracy in China: Political Reform in the Deng Xiaoping Era*, Cambridge, MA: Harvard University Press, 1994.

Kau, Michael Y. M. and John K. Leung (eds), *The Writings of Mao Zedong*, New York: Armonk, 1986.

Kraus, Richard Curt, *Brushes with Power: Modern Politics and the Chinese Art of Calligraphy*, Berkeley, CA: University of California Press, 1991.

Laing, Ellen Johnston, *The Winking Owl: Art in the People's Republic of China*, Berkeley, CA: University of California Press, 1998.

Leijonhufvud, Goran, *Going against the Tide: On Dissent and Big-character Posters in China* (Scandinavian Institute of Asian Studies monograph series no. 58), London: Curzon Press, 1990.

Link, Perry, *The Uses of Literature: Life in the Socialist Literary System*, Princeton, NJ: Princeton University Press, 2000.

Ma Wen-yee, *Snow Glistens on the Great Wall – The Complete Collection of Mao Tse-tung's Poetry*, Santa Barbara, CA: Santa Barbara Press, 1986.

MacFarquhar, Roderick, *The Hundred Flowers Campaign and the Chinese Intellectuals*, New York: Praeger, 1960.

MacFarquhar, Roderick, *The Origins of the Cultural Revolution, 1956–1966*, 3 vols, Oxford: Oxford University Press, 1974, 1983, 1997.

Miles, James, *The Legacy of Tiananmen*, Ann Arbor, MI: University of Michigan Press, 1996.

Perry, Elizabeth J. and Mark Selden (eds), *Chinese Society: Change, Conflict and Resistance*, London: Routledge, 2000.

Roberts, J. A. G., *A Concise History of China*, Cambridge, MA: Harvard University Press, 1999.

Salisbury, Harrison E., *The New Emperors: Mao and Deng – A Dual Biography*, London: HarperCollins, 1992.

Short, Philip, *Mao: A Life*, London: Hodder & Stoughton, 1999.

Zong Haiwen (ed.), *Years of Trial, Turmoil and Triumph – China from 1949 to 1988*, Beijing: Foreign Languages Press, 1989.

CHINESE BIBLIOGRAPHY

General 綜合

無名氏：現代書法：現代書畫學會書法首展作品選。北京：北京體育學院出版社，1986。

白謙慎：也論中國書法藝術的性質，書法研究，1982，第 2 期，28–40。

金學智：書法美學談。上海：上海書畫出版社，1984。

羅青：二十世紀書法美學之基礎，雄獅美術，第295期，56–63。

羅青：寫《白字》的方法，雄獅美術，第299期，92–7。

呂澎、易丹：中國現代藝術史。長沙：湖南美術出版社，1992，1995。

卜列平：中國現代派書法賞析 (An Appreciation of China Modernistic Calligraphers' Works)。成都：四川美術出版社，1993。

上海中國畫院：美術文集：上海中國畫院成立25周年紀念。上海：上海中國畫院，1985。

王南溟：理解現代書法：書法向現代藝術、向前衛藝術的轉型。南京：江蘇教育出版社，1994。

吳建賢編：上海書法家作品集。上海：上海書畫出版社，1979。

楊應時：巴蜀點兵：99成都20世紀末中國現代書法回顧 (Bashu Parade: '99 Chengdu Retrospective of Chinese Modern Calligraphy at the End of the 20th Century)。成都，1999。

楊朝嶺、陳筱鳳編：中國現代書法十年。南寧：廣西美術出版社，1996。

朱青生：中國現代書法初步概述，2000 [未出版文章]。

朱青生：關于現代書法的反書法性質，2000 [未出版文章]。

朱仁夫：中國現代書法史。北京：北京大學出版社，1996。

Chen Yi 陳毅

陳昊蘇編：陳毅詩詞全集。北京：華夏出版社，1993。

陳毅：陳毅詩稿。北京：文物出版社，1979。

陳小魯：記念陳毅。北京：文物出版社，1991。

朱祥金編：陳毅風范詞典。北京：中國檔案出版社，1995。

Deng Sanmu 鄧散木

鄧國治編：鄧散木印集。石家莊：河北美術出版社，1992。

鄧散木藝術陳列館編：鄧散木書刻藝術。哈爾濱：鄧散木藝術陳列館，1986。

郭若愚：南鄧北來新居處–漫談鄧散木的篆刻藝術，北方文物，1987，第2期 106–8，112。

Gu Gan 古干

無名氏：從具象到抽象–古干現代藝術小品。合肥：名畫家再創輝煌系列叢書，安徽美術出版社，1999。

古干：現代派–書法三步。北京：中國人民大學出版社，1992。

古干：古干三步。北京：華齡出版社，1996。

古干：古干書畫集。北京：中國文聯出版社，2000。

Guo Moruo 郭沫若

郭沫若：李白與杜甫。北京：人民文學出版社，1972。

郭沫若展：日中國交正常化20周年紀念、郭沫若生誕100周年記念（1992年11月7日–29日）。東京：日中友好會館美術館，1992。

郭平英編：郭沫若卷。二十世紀書法經典（張志欣、周聖英編）。石家莊：河北教育出版社、廣州：廣東教育出版社，1996。

郭庶英、郭平英、張澄寰編：郭沫若遺墨。石家莊：河北人民出版社，1980。

肖玫：郭沫若。北京：轉變中的近代中國（1840–1949）叢書，文物出版社，1992。

Han Yu 韓羽

韓羽：韓羽畫集。香港：榮寶齋（香港）有限公司，1990。

Huang Miaozi 黃苗子

黃苗子：黃苗子書法選 (Huang Miaozi's Calligraphy)。北京：中國友誼出版社，1988。

黃苗子：吳道子事輯。北京：中華書局，1991。

黃苗子：草書木蘭詞。香港：華寶齋書社有限公司，1995。

黃苗子：畫壇師友錄。臺北：滄海叢刊（美術），東大圖書公司，1998。

黃苗子：黃苗子書法。當代書法家精品集（張志欣、周聖英編）。石家莊：河北教育出版社、廣州：廣東教育出版社，1998.

黃苗子：黃苗子書古詩冊。香港：華寶齋書社，2000。

黃苗子、郁風：陌上花。南京：雙葉叢書，江蘇文藝出版社，1995。

黃苗子、郁風：2000 書畫集。上海：中國文化名人手稿館叢書，上海科學技術文獻出版社，2000。

李輝：風雨中的雕像。濟南：山東畫報出版社，1997，217–63（生死兩茫茫–黃苗子、郁風在"文革"中）。

李輝：人在旋渦–黃苗子與郁風。濟南：山東畫報出版社，1998。

如水編：三家詩。廣州：廣東教育出版社，1996，1–71（黃苗子：無腔集）。

楊朝嶺、陳筱鳳編，1996，同 上。

中國美術學院等編：黃苗子、郁風書畫展覽。杭州：中國美術學院陳列館，1994年11月。

Li Luogong 李駱公

丁伯奎：駝蹤。桂林：漓江出版社，1984（1986重印）。

范石甫：鐵筆撼山岳，方寸容天地–記現代書法篆刻家李駱公，現代書法，1996年，第9期，5–6。

高莽：駱公的篆刻，1997[未出版文章]。

楊朝嶺、陳筱鳳編，1996，同 上。

Lin Sanzhi 林散之

桂雍：潤含春雨，干裂秋風–林散之先生書藝述評，現代書法，1994年，第5期，3–4。

李漢章編：林散之草書中日友誼詩卷。合肥：安徽省美術出版社，1995。

林昌庚等：林散之。南京：江蘇文史資料第42輯，1991。

林散之：林散之書法選集。南京：江蘇美術出版社，1985，1994。

林散之：江上詩存。揚州：花山文藝出版社，1993。

林散之：林散之書法集。蘇州：古吳軒出版社，1997。

桑作楷：林散之卷。二十世紀書法經典（張志欣、周聖英編）。石家莊：河北教育出版社、廣州：廣東教育出版社，1996。

邵子退：種瓜軒詩稿。合肥：安徽文藝出版社，1994。

王冬齡編：林散之草書冊頁。杭州：中國美術學院出版社，1996。

Liu Zengfu 柳曾符

柳曾符：大學書法新編。上海：上海畫報出版社，1999。

柳曾符：一藝之成，源遠流長"記柳詒徵先生書法，書法研究，1985年，第2期（總第20輯），1–16。

柳曾符：柳曾符書學論文集。臺北：華正書局，1995。

柳曾符、張森：隸書基礎知識。上海：書法知識叢書，上海書畫出版社，1985，1990。

Mao Zedong 毛澤東

陳炳琛：回憶毛主席、周總理、朱委員長書法活動片段，書法，1980，第11期。

董志英：毛澤東逸事。北京：昆侖出版社，1989。

《毛主席手書選集》編輯委員會編：毛主席手書選集。北京，1967。

中共中央文獻研究室編：毛澤東詩詞集。北京：中央文獻出版社，1996。

中央檔案館編：毛澤東手書選集(一)：自作詩詞卷。北京：北京出版社，1993。

朱仁夫，1996，同上。

Pu Lieping 卜列平

卜列平：中國現代派書法賞析（An Appreciation of China Modernistic Calligraphers' Works）。成都：四川美術出版社，1993。

Qi Gong 啟功

侯剛：啟功卷。當代書法家精品集（張志欣、周聖英編）。石家莊：河北教育出版社，廣州：廣東教育出版社，1998。

啟功：論書絕句。北京：三聯書店，1990。

啟功：啟功書畫留影冊。北京：北京師范大學出版社，1992。

啟功：啟功草書千字文。北京：中國和平出版社，1994。

啟功：啟功叢稿，詩詞卷。北京：中華書局，1999。

朱仁夫，1996，同上。

Sa Benjie 薩本介

薩本介作品（椅子系列），江蘇畫刊（Jiangsu Art Monthly），1996年，第1期，39。

Sha Menghai 沙孟海

劉新：翰墨人生–書法大師沙孟海的前半生。杭州：浙江文藝出版社，1994。

駱恒光：當代書壇大師沙孟海–記沙孟海的書藝道路，現代書法，1994年，第6期，6–7，11。

沙更世、沙茂世編：沙孟海卷。二十世紀書法經典（張志欣、周聖英編）。石家莊：河北教育出版社、廣州：廣東教育出版社，1996。

沙匡世編：沙孟海年表。杭州：西泠印社，2000。

沙孟海：沙孟海真行草書集。上海：上海書畫出版社，1994。

上海書畫出版社編：沙孟海書法集。上海：上海書畫出版社，1987，1994。

孫曉泉：博學善書老當益壯–西子湖畔聆著名書法家沙孟海談心得[無來源]。西泠藝叢，1992年，第2期（沉痛悼念沙孟海先生）。

Shen Yinmo 沈尹默

馬保杰編：沈尹默卷。二十世紀書法經典（張志欣、周聖英編）。石家莊：河北教育出版社、廣州：廣東教育出版社，1996。

沈尹默：沈尹默法書集。上海：上海書畫出版社，1981，1994。

沈尹默：尹默法書。西安：三秦出版社，1991。

沈尹默：沈尹默書毛澤東詩詞。杭州：浙江人民美術出版社，1992。

沈尹默：沈尹默書小草千字文。北京：中國和平出版社，1993。

沈尹默：沈尹默小楷。南京：江蘇古籍出版社，1997。

沈尹默、吳玉如：沈尹默、吳玉如書毛澤東詩詞三十七首。天津：天津古籍出版社，1993。

張曉明編：沈尹默手稿墨跡。上海：上海書畫出版社，1999。

朱仁夫，1996，同上。

Wang Dongling 王冬齡

宋忠元編：王冬齡書畫集（The art works of Wang Dong Ling/Wang Dong Ling Calligraphy and Paintings）。杭州：中國美術學院出版社，1994。

王冬齡：書法藝術。杭州：美術教材叢書，浙江美術學院出版社，1986（1988第2版，1992重印）。

王冬齡：王冬齡草書唐詩三十首。合肥：中國當代名家系列叢帖，安徽教育出版社，1998。

王冬齡：書法篆刻。杭州：高等藝術教育"九五"部級教材，中國藝術教育大系，美術卷（Chinese Art Education Encyclopaedia, Fine Arts Series）中國美術學院出版社，1999。

謝海：王冬齡，我書故我在，美術報（China Art Weekly），2001年3月24日，8–9。

Wang Nanming 王南溟

王南溟：理解現代書法：書法向現代藝術、向前衛藝術的轉型，南京：江蘇教育出版社，1994。

Wang Shixiang 王世襄

王世襄：錦灰堆：王世襄自選集。北京：生活、讀書、新知三聯書店，1999。

Wei Ligang 魏立剛

魏立剛：魏立剛書法篆刻集。太原：山西人民出版社，1991。

魏立剛：[序]偽大師（Predent [sic] Great–Artist: A collection of Four Children's Calligraphy）。太原：爾漁館，1999。

魏立剛：漢字維度（Chinese Characters – Measure），北京：楊煒志，2000。

Yang Xianyi 楊憲益

如水編：三家詩。廣州：廣東教育出版社，1996，72–139（楊憲益：彩虹集）。

楊憲益：銀翹集。香港：天地圖書有限公司（Cosmos Books Ltd），1995。

Ye Gongchuo 葉恭綽

黃苗子：畫壇師友錄。臺北：東大圖書公司，1998，65–72（因蜜尋花–葉恭綽談書法）。

劉紹唐：民國人物小傳。臺北：傳記文學雜志社，第二冊，233–5。

啟功：序，1987 [無來源]。

葉恭紹：跋，1987[無來源]。

張大千：序葉遐庵書畫選集。臺灣[無日期]。

Zhang Dawo 張大我

楊朝嶺、陳筱鳳，1996，同上。

張大我：從書法《飛出紙面》談起，2000年國際書法交流臺北大展論文集（歐宗智編），中國書法學會，臺北，2000。

Zhang Ding 張仃

李兆忠：畢加索的中國知音（An understanding friend of Picaso [sic] in China），中國與世界（The World and China），1999年，第5期（總第61期），28–9。

楊朝嶺、陳筱鳳，1996，同上。

Zhang Qiang 張強

陳傳席編：張強，首卷：蹤跡背景。北京：中國當代先鋒藝術家研究叢書（Chinese Avant–Garde Artists Research Series）（二），中國華僑出版社，1997。

陳孝信編：行為書寫：張強蹤跡藝術。濟南：捌佰蹤跡館，2001。

文備、張強：現代書法十周年文獻匯編。南寧：廣西美術出版社，1998。

張強：迷離錯置的影響–現代藝術在中國的文化視點（Images in Disorder – The Cultural Point of View of Modern Art in China）。濟南：藝術大視野叢書，山東美術出版社，1998。

張強：中國畫論：系統論。中華人民共和國文化部九五規劃–全國高等藝術院校（美術）研究生（本科生）通用教材（The System of Chinese Painting Theory [Textbook for postgraduate art students throughout China, which is part of the Ninth Five–year Plan of the Culture Ministry of the People's Republic of China]），南京：江蘇美術出版社，1998。

Zhang Sen 張森

上海中國畫院畫廊編：張森。上海：上海中國畫院畫家作品叢書（The Artists' Works Series of Shanghai Traditional Chinese Painting Academy），上海畫報出版社，1998。

張森：張森隸書滕王閣序。上海：上海書店，1990，1991。

張森：張森書法藝術。上海：學林出版社，1992。

張森：張森隸書岳陽樓記。上海：上海畫報出版社，1996。

張森、柳曾符：隸書基礎知識。上海：書法知識叢書，上海書畫出版社，1985，1990。

張森等：當代書家五體千字文。上海：上海書店出版社，1997。

祝敏申編：大學書法。上海：復旦大學出版社，1985，1993。

Zhang Zhengyu 張正宇

沈鵬編：張正宇書法選。北京：人民美術出版社，1979。

沈鵬：前言（二）–書法闊通書法津，1982[無來源]。

王朝聞：前言（一），1982 [無來源]。

楊朝嶺、陳筱鳳，1996，同上。

張正宇：張正宇書畫選集。北京：人民美術出版社，1985。

283

INDEX

Page numbers in italics refer to illustrations.

abstract art 33, 36, 37, 38, 56, 65, 125, 167, 186, 87, 190, 192, 224, 231–3, 243, 244–9, 258, 262
abstract expressionism 56, 235, 258
acrylic paints 37, 191, 242, 247
Admonitions of the Palace Instructress (scroll) 152, 160
Archaeology (journal) 45, 87
archaic script 174, 176, 178
art colleges 59, 64–5
Art Forum (journal) 254
Australia 178, 179–80, 227, 230, 235
  aboriginal art 181
autumn 185, 213–14
Avant-Garde calligraphy 11, *13*, 15, 36–9, 56–8, 61–2, 65, 131, 226–63

Bai Qianshen 37, 56, 56
Bai Yunshu 237
balls of calligraphy (Wang Nanming) 37, 62, *62*, 252–3, *254*, 255, *255*
bamboo strips 19, 20, 78, 229, 251
Bank of China, logo 46, 83
'Bashu Parade', *see* 'Retrospective of Chinese Modern Calligraphy at the End of the Twentieth Century'
Beijing 151, 173–4
  Beijing Hotel 45
  Central Academy of Fine Arts 65, 182
  Chairman Mao Memorial Hall 52
  exhibitions 53, 127, 165, 169, 180
  Forbidden City 46, 88
  Gong Wang Fu 146, 147
  Great Hall of the People 137
  Guo Moruo's name plaques 83
  Martyrs' Memorial 45, 52, *52*, 109–10
  China National Art Gallery 110, 169, 174 (*see also* Modernist Calligraphy Exhibition)

pageants and parades 119
Palace Museum 68, 76, 83, 109
Rong Bao Zhai (art shop) 46, 76, 82, 83, 111, 114, 137, 216, 217, 222, 233
Song Feng Xuan Gallery 242, 247
Temple of Everlasting Peace 149
Tiananmen Square 45, 52, 110, 175
  demonstrations (1989) 53–4, 58, 178, 185, 217, 271
  Qing Ming Festival 52, 267
University 109, 147, 152, 154
Wang Dongling's exhibitions 165, 169
big-character posters 46, 47, 48, *49*, 54, 114, 163, 211, 244, 266
'bird' script 230
Böll, Heinrich 186
boxes (frames), for characters *22–3*, 37, 149, 239, 247–8
Brehmer, Professor K.P. 184
bronze script (*jinwen*) (on bronzes) 18, 19, 22, 121, 125, 181, 230
brushes 17, 20, 23, 24, *24*, *25*, 46, 185
  Li Luogong's 127
  Mao Zedong's 106, 108
brushwork *26*
  Chen Yi 94, 95
  Guo Moruo ('counter-movement') 82
  Han Yu 214
  Li Luogong 127
  Liu Zengfu 204, 206–7
  Mao Zedong 106, 115–17
  Pu Lieping 241
  Sa Benjie 222, 224
  Sha Menghai 136
  Shen Yinmo 26, *27*, 70
  Wang Dongling 169–70
  Wei Ligang 246, 247, 248
  Zhang Dawo 230, 231
  Zhang Sen 34, *35*, 200

Zhang Zhengyu 122
Buddhism 22, 23, 74, 76, 225, 237, 244–5
  Gu Gan 32, 185, 187
  Lin Sanzhi 140, *144–5*, 145
  Taiwan exhibition 161

cadre schools 147, 156–7, 161, 217
Cai Yong 230
Caishiji 140, 145, 151
calligraphers' associations 44, 59, 196, 202, 209; *see also* Chinese Calligraphers' Association
Cao Cao, *The Indomitable Soul 115*, 116, *128–9*, 129
Cartoonists' Club 173, 181
cartoons and cartoonists 119, 172–3, 210, 211, 212, 213, 244
cats 119, 121, 124, 212
Central Academy of Design 53
Central Academy of Culture and History 71
Château Mouton Rothschild label 61, *61*, 182, 189–90
Chen Bingchen 42
Chen Duxiu 67
Chen Shuliang 53
Chen Yi 91–9, 101, 216, 269
  and Guo Moruo 82, 83, 93, 95
  and Liu Yizheng 203
  and Mao 91–2, 95–8
  patronage of Shen Yinmo 67, 68–9, 71, 93
  and Zhou Enlai 95, 96, 98
  Chengdu 93–4, *94*
  Kunming 96–7, *96*
  Mount Mogan 92, 93
  Qingdao 93, 94, *94*
  Red Leaves of the Western Hills 97, 99, 144
Chengdu
  exhibitions 62, 191, 242, 261
  International Exchange Centre 237, 242
Chiang Kaishek, *see* Jiang Jieshi
children 19, *22*, 37, *43*, 64, *64*, 101, 239, 247–8, 252–3

China National Academy of Fine Arts, *see under* Hangzhou
China National Art Museum/ Gallery, *see under* Beijing
Chinese Academy of Sciences 46, 52, 81, 204
Chinese Calligraphers' Association 44, 53–4, 60, 137, 150, 168, 201, 202, 245
Chinese Contemporary Calligraphy Exhibition (1991), Shanghai 61–2, 251–2
Chinese People's Political Consultative Conference (CPPCC) 69, 137, 144, 150–1, 158–9, 175, 271, 272
Chongqing 68, 134, 173
Chu Suiliang 68, 77
Classical calligraphy (Classicism) 11, *12*, 15, 25–8, 33, 39, 60, 71, *85*, 105, 132–61, 164, 196
classical texts 23, 27, 46, 47, 54, 69, 78, 83, 108, 144, 157, 163, 200, 237
clerical script (*li shu*) 17, *18*, 19, 20, 78, 100, 164, 174, 196, 206, 221
  Zhang Sen 34, 35, 197
collages 55, 165, 167–8, 171
Cologne (Germany), exhibition 178, 186
Communists and Communist Party 23, 27, 67, 68, 75, 76, 77, 80, 81, 91, 92, 93, 100, 106, 108, 113, 120, 130, 134, 141, 144, 147, 154, 173, 182, 203, 210, 211, 265, 266, 271
Confucianism 23
Confucius 84, 89, 147, 180, 205, 207, 238
'counter-movement' brush technique 82
Cubism 55, 184
Cultural Revolution 47–50, 52, 53, 54, 55, 113–15, 116
  and Chen Yi 97–9
  Classicists 27

Gu Gan 182
Guo Moruo 86–90
Han Yu 211
Huang Miaozi 174
Li Luogong 127, 130
Lin Sanzhi 142, 143, 144, 145
Liu Zengfu 203, 204, 209
Modernists 29
Pu Lieping 236
Qi Gong 147–8
Sa Benjie 216–17
Sha Menghai 136–7
Shen Yinmo 69, 72–3
Wang Dongling 55, 163–4
Wang Nanming 250
Wang Shixiang 155–7, 161
Wei Ligang 244
Yang Xianyi 266–7
Ye Gongchuo 79
Zhang Dawo 228
Zhang Sen 196
Zhang Zhengyu 120–1, 122, 123
cursive script (*cao shu*) 17, *18*, 19, 23, 237
    by Deng Sanmu 100, 101, *102–3*
    by Gu Gan 185
    by Huang Miaozi 174
    by Lin Sanzhi 141, 144, 165
    by Mao Zedong 47, *110*, 111, 112, 237
    by Shen Yinmo 70
    by Wang Dongling 166, 168, 169, 171
    by Zhang Qiang 259
    see also wild cursive script

Da Guan Lou Pavilion, inscription 122–3
Da Jiangshang 207
Da Xiong Bao Dian pavilion, Hangzhou, name plaque 44, *45*, 134–5, 136, 137
dance 15, 111, *111*
Daodejing 170
Daoism 23, 169, 170–1, *170–1*, 186, 221, 237, 261–2
deconstruction 252
Deng Sanmu 27, 43, 100–4
Deng Xiaoping 29, 53, 58, 73, 114, 131, 137, 144, 150, 158, 175, 179, 186, 196, 204, 237, 244, 270, 271
    calligraphy by 59
    praised Guo Moruo 90
Derrida, Jacques 252

Ding Cong 266
Dong Qichang 21, *21*, 148–9
draft script 20, 22
Du Fu 88, 205
Du Mu
    Drinking Fen Wine 246
    Going up the Hill 142–3, 144
Dunhuang 32, 187

earthquake 123
elephant 176
'Exploring Modern Calligraphy' exhibition, Beijing 169

Fan Guan *268*, 269
Fan Li 197
Fauves 51, 125
'flying white' script *63*, 230, 231
folk art 119, 211, 242
Forbidden City, *see* Beijing
'four treasures' 23–4, *24*
Fu Xinian 152, 160
furniture calligraphy 218–20, 224

Gang of Four 51, 52, *52*, 89, 90, 97, 99, 114, 121, 122, 124, 130, 136, 144, 148, 175, 267, *268*, 269
Gao Mang *131*
Geng Biao 64
Germany
    influence of Wang Dongling 171
    artists in China 254
    exhibitions in 178, 255
    visit by Gu Gan 186–7
    visit by Huang Miaozi 178
'ghosts and monsters' 130
gongfu 170
'Grand Tradition' 11, 34, 60, 66–117, 197, 215
grass script *21*, 70, 84, 183
Great Leap Forward 52, 82, 112, 116, 174, 233
Greenwich, Royal Observatory 181, 190
Gu Gan 55, 65, 124, 131, 182–93, 252, 257
    book (1986) 184, 238
    and Huang Miaozi 178, 183, 186
    label for Château Mouton Rothschild 61, *61*, 182, 189–90
    seals carved by 32, 187
    and Zhang Zhengyu 122
    A Wish for Universal Peace 186

The Age of Red and Gold 190–1, *192–3*
Alone in a Vast Wasteland 187
Catching up with Time 190
Crying Deer 185
'mountain' (*shan*) 30, *31*
The Mountains are Breaking Up 55, 184
My Heart goes out of the Window 188–9
Opening Up 188, *189*
The Preciousness of Peace 185
Walking Alone 187, *188*
World of Supreme Bliss 30, *32*, 185
Gu Kaizhi 152
Gu Wenda 65
Guangzhou 149
Guilin 127, 129, 130, 131
Guo Moruo 46, 68, 80–90, 134
    admiration for Qi Gong 148
    and Chen Yi 82, 83, 93, 95
    disliked by Jiang Qing and the Gang of Four 88–9, 89, 90
    and Huang Miaozi 173
    Japanese calligraphy 50, 81
    and Li Luogong 126, 127
    and Lin Sanzhi 140, 142–3, 145
    and Liu Zengfu 204
    and Mao Zedong 45, 79, 81–2, 83–4, 85, 86–7, 88, 89, 111
    and Zhou Enlai 51, 80, 81, 82, 87, 89–90

halo effect 31, *33*
Han dynasty 78
    bamboo strips 251
    brushwork 125
    scripts 19, 20, 196, 246
    tiles 230
Han Yu 34, 117, 124, 210–15
    Falling Leaves 212–13, 213–14
    Rhyme-Prose on Literature 214
    Rise up Towards the Sun 214–15, 215
Hangzhou 133, 136, 137, 138, 202
    China National Academy of Fine Arts 29, 65, 135, 164–5, 169, 171
    exhibitions 165
    Su Causeway (*Su Di*) 137, 138
    Zhejiang Museum 134
    see also Da Xiong Bao Dian pavilion

heart *61*, 187, 189, 190
Heinrich Böll Institute 178, 186
Hong Kong 46, 76, 172, 205, 206, 255
    Arts Development Council 254
    British handover 272–3
Hong Peimo 250
Hua Guofeng 52–3
Huaisu, monk *20, 21*, 100, 111, 122, 237
Huang Binhong 140
Huang Miaozi 27, 131, 159, 172–81
    and Gu Gan 178, 183, 186
    and Han Yu 212
    and Yang Xianyi 266, 267, 269, 270, 272
    and Ye Gongchuo 75, 174
    and Zhang Zhengyu 121, 122, 124, 174, 175
    couplet about Tiananmen Square 53, 175
    The Gentlemanly Scholar 179–80, *180*
    Great Changes 176, *177*, 180
    Mit diesen Händen exhibition 178, 180, 186
    The Night Feast 180–1, 181
    The Rain-filled Clouds 179, *179*, 180
    scrolls *174–5*, 175
    seven scripts 18
Huang Yongyu 159, 266, 269, 270, *270*, *271*
Hunan Provincial Calligraphers' Association 59
'Hundred Flowers Movement' 46, *47*, 76, 81, 101, 147, 173, 266

illiteracy 42–3
ink 21, 24–5, 94
    coloured 31, 183
    'dark' 25, 31
    'overnight' 25, 185, 187
    red 25
    used by the Avant-Garde 37, 38, 229, 231–3, 249, *249*
    used by Classicists 26, 70
    used by Modernists 29, 30, 31, *32–3*, 169, 171, 177, 183, 191
    used by Neo-Classicists 34
    'wet' and 'damp' 25, 31
inksticks 21, 24, *24*
inkstones 21, 24–5, *24*
installations 37, *39*, 57–8, *57*, 255, 262

Internet website 235
'iron line' script 142, 143, 144, 145, *170*

Japan 71
  attacks on and occupation of China 100–1, 126, 154, 172, 173
  calligraphy 50, 54, 71, 81, 143, 144–5, 175–6, 206
  diplomatic relations with China 50, 71, 89, 127, 142–3, 148
  exhibitions 71, 127
  Guo Moruo 71, 80–1, 89
  Huang Miaozi's visits 175–6
  occupation of Shanghai 68, 92, 101
  Wang Dongling's sabbatical in 166, 169
  Ye Gongchuo in 74
Jia Dao 117
Jia Yu Guan gate 202
Jiang Jieshi (Chiang Kaishek) 22, 74, 81, 83, 92, 108, 133, 134, 135, 136, 138, 141, 173, 265
Jiang Kui 207, *208*
Jiang Qing 51, 109, 122, 124, 148, 157, 266
  attacked Li Luogong 51, 128–9, 130
  and Chen Yi 97, 99
  disliked Guo Moruo 89
  exhibition of 'black works of art' 51
  and Huang Miaozi 174
  and the owls 269
Jiang Zemin 99
  public inscriptions by *58*, 59
  sign for Caishiji museum by 145
  title inscription by 114

Kandinsky, Vassily 182, 183, 257
Kang Sheng 45, 87
Kang Youwei 22, 133, 251
Kissinger, Dr Henry 50, 98
Klee, Paul 56, 163, 186, 258

Laozi 90, 170
Li Bai 78, 88, 140, 145
  inspiration for Gu Gan 55, 184
  Invitation to Wine 116–17
  The Night Feast 180–1, 181, *241*

The Song of Mount Lu 116
Li Henian 227, 245
Li Ji (the 'Book of Rites') 205
Li Luogong 29, 55, 125–31
  and the Fauves 51, 125
  Da Gui 130
  'I lost my proud poplar' 51, *51*, 128
  The Indomitable Soul 128–9, 129–30, *130*
Li Shutong 22, 217, 222
Lin Biao 49, 89, 97, 98
Lin Kai 268, *269*
Lin Sanzhi 54, 89, 140–5, 148, 196
  cursive script 141, 144, 165
  'iron line' script 142, 143, 144, 145, *170*
  memorial museum 145, 151
  Wang Dongling's teacher 142, 144, 164, 165, 169, 170, *170*
  Going up the Hill 142–3, 144
  Huichang (by Mao) 50, 143
  Sheng Tian Cheng Fo 145
Lippincott, Kristen 181
Liu Chang 205
Liu Gongquan 148
Liu Haisu 125
Liu Xin 136
Liu Yazi 79, 87, 109
Liu Yizheng 203, 205, 206, 207, 209
Liu Yuxi, *Reply to Bai Juyi* 117
Liu Zengfu 27, 134, 203–9, 250
  book written with Zhang Sen 197, 206
  brushwork 204, 206–7
  and Chen Yi 203
  taught by Shen Yinmo 26, 72, 203–4, 206
London
  Royal Academy exhibition (1936) 75
  Spencer House exhibition 190
Long Chang Si Bei 169
Lu Ji 214
Lu Jian 269
Lu Weizhao 29, 164
Lu Xun 43, 121
Lu You 69
Lushan (Mount Lu) 116

Mao Zedong 42–3, 44, 45, 46–8, 105–17
  brushwork 115–17
  and Chen Yi 91–2, 95–8
  couplet by 124

cursive and wild cursive script by 47, *110*, 111, 112, 237
  death of 52–3, 124
  and Guo Moruo 45, 79, 81–2, 83–4, 85, 86–7, 88–9, 111
  'Little Red Books' 114
  newspaper mastheads 113
  poems by 27, 83, 84, 91–2, 111–12, 113, 122, 142
  running script by 106, 107, 110
  Sa Benjie's copies of poems by 217
  scrolls by Sha Menghai 136–7
  and Shen Yinmo 69, 70, 71, 72
  statues of 99
  and Yang Xianyi 266
  and Ye Gongchuo 45, 74, 75–6, 79, 87, 109
  and Zhang Zhengyu 119, 120
  Beidaihe 112, 135
  Hong Qi ('The Red Flag') *110*, 111
  Huichang ('A dawn breaks in the East') 50, 106–7, *107*, 143
  'I lost my proud poplar' 51, *51*, 85, 125, 128
  The Indomitable Soul 115, 116
  Invitation to Wine 116–17
  The Long March 112, *112*
  The Loushan Pass 70
  Manjianghong 83, 84, 113, 116, 120
  Mount Liupan 47, 48, 112, 114
  Ode to a Plum Blossom 123
  Reascending Jingkangshan 136–7
  Reply to Bai Juyi 117
  Reply to Mr Liu Yazi 112
  The Song of Mount Lu 116
  Swimming 113
  see also Cultural Revolution; Great Leap Forward
Matisse, Henri 39, 56, 61, 163, 164, 182
May Fourth Movement 23, 67, 93
Mi Fu 21, *21*, 68, 148–9, 207, 237
miaomo 232, 233, 235
Ming dynasty 21, 23, 117, 120
  paper 24
Miró, Joan 33, 163, 182, 183, 186, 258
Mit diesen Händen ('With these

Hands') exhibition 178, 180, 186
Modernist calligraphy 11, *13*, 15, 29–33, 34, 54, 55, 55, 56, 60–1, 65, 131, 145, 162–93, 229, 238, 246, 257
Modernist Calligraphy Exhibition, Beijing (1985) 55, 55, 131, 165, 176, 183–4, 229, 245
Montgomery, Viscount 113
moon *18*, 176
Moore, Henry 37, 235
Mount Kunlun 178
Mount Taishan 87, *87*
Mount Yanzi 121
'mountain' (*shan*) *18*, 30, *31*
music 15, 27, *28–9*, 70, 166, 233, 239–40

Nanjing 61, 141, 143, 144–5
  Modernist exhibition 188
National Academy of Fine Arts, *see under* Hangzhou
Nationalist Party 22–3, 74, 80, 109, 133, 134, 138
nature 174, 185, 228, 230–1, 232, 237, 247
Neo-Classical calligraphy 11, *13*, 15, 33–6, 60, 65, 194–225
New China 27, 41–4, 69, 102, 108
Ningbo 133, 138
Nixon, President Richard 50, 88
Northern Wei dynasty 74, 78, 244, 245
  Buddhist statues 74
  stone inscriptions 251

oil paints 37, 191, 247
oracle-bone script (*jiaguwen*) *18*, 19, 22, 125, 180, 185, 187, 204, 205, 206, 239, 240, 242, 246
Orchid Pavilion Preface 21, 81, 137
Ou Chu, Party official 148, 149
Ouyang Xiu 249
Ouyang Xun 49, 148, 160, 161

palaces 41, 45
Pan Jijiong 268, *269*
paper 17, 23, 24, *24*, 99, 150, 190, 191, 249
  xuan 24, 37, 191, 242
pens 46, 59, 106, 246
People's China 50, 89, 142, 148

People's Daily 45, 79, 90, 108

photography 235

Picasso, Pablo 39, 56, 61, 163, 164, 171, 182, 239

   met Zhang Ding 29, 53, 54

pictograms 16, 17, 22, 30, 36, 38, 51, 121, 125, 127, 185, 190, 229, 242, 258, 179, *179*

political calligraphy 46–53

post-Impressionism 125

Pu Lieping 236–43

   gallery opened by 242, 247

   Autumn Wind 239, *240*

   Dreams 241, *242*

   The Future is Bright, but... 242, *243*

   Music at Dawn 239

   Pastoral Melodies 36, *38*, 239–40

Pu Ru, Prince 146

Pu Zhao Temple, Mount Taishan 87, *87*

Qi Baishi 22, 43, 217, 218, 225

Qi Gong 26–7, 53, 54, 60, *60*, 143, 144, 146–52, 266

   auction 201

   Caishiji museum's name board by 145, 151

   Guo Moruo's admiration for 148

   running script 27, 148, 150

   scrolls for Ou Chu *148–9*, 149–50

   seal by 147

   vertical grid by 27, *28*

   and Wang Shixiang 152, 159, 160

   and Ye Gongchuo 75, 76, 77

Qian Long emperor 108, 207

Qiao Guanhua 49

Qin, First Emperor 19

Qing dynasty 20, 22, 23

Qiu Zhengzhong 37, 54

Qu Yuan 121, 157, 266

Rauschenberg, Robert 57

Red Guards 48, 49–50, *50*, 54, 72–3, 79, 97, 98, 103, 114, 121, 136, 142, 147, 155–6, 158, 163, 182, 211, 228, 236, 266

regular script (*kai shu*) 17, *18*, 19, 20, *20*, 21, *21*, 45, 69, 134, 135, 148, 169, 183, 237, 246, 258

reshaping characters 30–1, *31*

'Retrospective of Chinese Modern Calligraphy at the End of the Twentieth Century' (exhibition, Chengdu, 1999) 62, 191, 242, 261–2

Rong Bao Zhai, *see under* Beijing

Rothschild, Baroness Philippine de 189; *see also* Château Mouton Rothschild

Rousseau, Jean-Jacques 223

Ruan Ji 56, 166

running script (*xing shu*) 17, *18*, *19*

   by Chen Yi 92

   by Deng Sanmu 100

   by Dong Qichang 21, *21*, 148–9

   by Liu Zengfu 204, 206

   by Mao Zedong 45, 106, 107, 110

   by Qi Gong 27, 148, 150

   by Sa Benjie 221

   by Shen Yinmo 70

   by Wang Dongling 169

   by Wang Shixiang 161

   by Wang Xianzhi 135

   by Wang Xizhi 20, *20*, 100

   by Zhang Sen 197, 200

   by Zhang Zhengyu 120

Sa Benjie 50, 161, 216–25

   couplet *36–7*, 221

   furniture calligraphy 218–20, 224

   jue and *wu* characters blended 31, *32*, 225

   Mao's poems copied out by 217

   seal script 220, 223

   and Wang Shixiang 160, 161, 218

   A Fable about a Table 160, 218, *219*

   A Talk between Friends 218

   Let Yourself Go 222, *223*

   Realization 225, *225*

'Sacred Mountains' exhibition, New York (1993) 167

Sanjing Mountain 202

Sanxi Tang Fatie 108

Schubert, Franz 239

sculptures, calligraphic 37, 55, 235, 253

seal script (*zhuan shu*) 10, 19, 22, 45, 78, 100, 164, 201

   by Gu Gan 183

   by Huang Miaozi 176, 178, 180

   by Sa Benjie 220, 223

   by Zhang Zhengyu 120, 121

   large *18*, *19*

   small *18*, *19*

   seals 25, 106

   by Deng Sanmu 102, 103

   by Gu Gan 32, 187

   by Li Luogong 125, 126, 127

   by Qi Gong 147

   by Sha Menghai 133, 137

   by Ye Gongchuo 75

Sha Menghai 27, 53, 54, 133–9

   Da Xiong Bao Dian pavilion name plaque by 45, 134–5, 136, 137

   scrolls for Mao Zedong 136–7

   seal carving by 133, 137

   Wang Dongling taught by 164

   The Joys of Spring 138, *139*

Shanghai 119, 172–3, 181, 250, 251

   Airport *48*, 114

   Calligraphers' Association 44, 196, 202, 209

   Chen Yi, mayor of 67, 68–9, 92–3, 101

   Chinese Contemporary Calligraphy Exhibition (1991) 61–2, 251–2

   Chinese Painting Academy 71, 76, 196–7

   Deng Sanmu 100–1, 103

   Dresdner Bank 201

   exhibitions 53, 60, 196

   Fudan University 205, 206

   Historical and Cultural Research Institute 76, 78, 92

   Japanese occupation 68, 92, 101

   Longhua Temple 135

   Municipal Museum and Library 93, 94, 95

   museum 137, 159–60, 218

   name plaques 59

   Shen Yinmo 67, 68–9, 71, 72, 93

   Zhang Sen's calligraphy 202

Shang-Zhou period 178

Shao Yanxiang 272

Shaolin monastery 140, 170

Shaoxing, memorial temple of Wang Xizhi 137

Shen Yinmo 43, 44, 67–73, 77, 196

   brushwork 26, *27*, 70

   Chen Yi's patronage 67, 68–9, 71, 93

Liu Zengfu's teacher 26, 72, 203–4, 206

   and Mao 69, 70, 71, 72

   museum 137

   Wang Xizhi's letters copied by 69, 70–1, *70–1*

   and Zhou Enlai 71, 72, 73

   Zao Ji 70

Shi Lu 30

Shi Tao 34, 124

Shu Tong 53

silk 24

'simplified' characters 101

Six Dynasties 70

Society of Modern Calligraphy 184

Song dynasty 21, 36, 141

Song Feng Xuan Gallery, Beijing 242, 247

Song Qingling, Madam 79, 87

Southern Song dynasty 200

Soviet Union 50, 65, 84, 88, 95, 113, 120, 186

stone inscriptions 20, 22, 78, 109, 121, 213, 246, 251

streets and shop signs 41, *41*

Su Dongpo 94

Sui dynasty 70

Sun Boxiang 245

Sun Guoting 26, 100

Sun Zhongshan (Sun Yatsen) 74, 87, 172

Sunset Pass 159, 202

Suzhou 133

taiji balls 261–2

Taiwan 13, 57, 88, 161

Taiyuan 245

Tang dynasty 16

   brushwork 251

   poetry 36, 49, 70, 159

   scripts 19, 20

Tapiès, Antoni 190, 258

Temple of Confucius, Qufu 84, 158, 202

temples 41, 45

The Thousand Character Essay 201

Tian Wang Dian pavilion, name plaque 135

Tibet 178, 183, 242

tiger *18*, 31, *167*, 242

Tokyo (Japan), Ziguba University 206

'traceology' 256, 258–63

United States of America 57, 65, 98, 166–8, 171, 186

287

vertical columns, of characters 20, *26*, 34
vertical grid, by Qi Gong 27, *28*
videos 37, 62, 246, 253
Vlaminck, Maurice de 125

Wang Bo 201
Wang Dongling 54, 55, 163–71
  collages 55, 165, 167–8, 171
  cursive script 166, 168, 169, *171*
  Lin Sanzhi as teacher of 142, 144, 164, 165, 169, 170, *170*
  Sha Menghai as teacher of 164
  and Western art 165, 166–7
  Feeling and Passion 168, *169*
  Mount Tai 56, 166
  Ru, Dao, Fo 166
  Tiger 167
  'View from Heaven' 166
Wang Nanming 54, 62, 250–5
  balls as furniture 255, *255*
  'Black Series' 251–2, *252*
  Combination: Balls of Characters 37, 62, *62*, 252–3, *254*
Wang Shixiang 27, 152, 153–61, 174, 266
  poem by *26*, 157, 161
  and Sa Benjie 160, 161, 218
  scrolls 272, *272–3*
  Returning 158–9, 159
Wang Wei 35, 159, *206–7*
Wang Xiaju 217
Wang Xianzhi 68, 135
Wang Xizhi 20, *20*, 68, 81, 92, 100, 161, 201
  letters copied by Shen Yinmo 69, 70–1, *70–1*
  memorial temple at Shaoxing 137
Wang Xuezhong 245
Warring States period 197

water buffalo 156, *156–7*
Wei dynasties 78, 251
Wei Ligang 37, 242, 244–9
  'Wei's squares' 37, *246–7, 247–9*
    Wisteria Sinensis 13, 248, *248*
Wen Tingyun 197, *198–9*
Western art 29, 53, 56–7, 61, 125, 183–4, 249, 261
  abstract 33, 36, 125, 192, 258
  abstract expressionism 56, 235, 258
  avant-garde 29
  exhibitions 53
  and Wang Dongling 165, 166–7
Western Han period, paper 24
Whitman, Walt 239, *240*
wild cursive script 20, *20*, 47, 122, 246
  by Deng Sanmu 101, *102–3*
  by Mao Zedong 47, 111, 112
  see also cursive script
Women's Art in the Twentieth Century exhibition (1998) 260
'worm' script 230
Wu Changshuo 22, 133, 137
Wu Shanzhuan, 'Red Room' 39
Wu Sichang 269
Wu Yi mountains 85–6, *86*
Wu Yuru 227
Wu Zuguang 270

Xi Ling Seal-Carving Society 137, 138
Xia Wanchun 94–5
Xia Yongyi 94–5
Xian 209, 213
Xiao Tiean 100
Xin Qiji 200, *200–1*
Xu Bing 36–7, 57, *57*
Xu Wei 165
xuan paper 24, 37, 191, 242

Yan Zhenqing 20, *20*, 49, 77, 80, 135
Yang Jiang 254
Yang Xianyi 121, 175, 265–73
Yangzhou, Slender West Lake pavilion 207
Ye Gongchuo 43, 74–9, 147
  and Huang Miaozi 75, 174
  and Mao Zedong 45, 74, 75–6, 79, 87, 109
  seal by 75
  Escapism 78
Ye Jianying 124
Yi Bingshou 36, *36–7*, 100, 221, 222
Youth Palaces 44, 64
Yu Feng 121, 122, 173, 174, 175, 178, 179, 180–1
Yu Youren 22–3, 68, 77, 211–12, 217
Yuan dynasty 21

Zao Weifang 100
Zen Buddhism 23, 140, 169, 225, 229
Zhang Dawo 37, 227–35
  'flying white' script *63*, 230, 231
  Black Moon 232–3, 232
  Dragon 231, 231
  Letter 233, 234
  Love Letters 233
  Sex between Heaven and Earth 235
  The Volume (Ce) 229
Zhang Ding 29, 53, 54
Zhang Qiang 36, 37, 62, 256–63
  'traceology' 256, 258–63
Zhang Sen 34, 195–202
  book written with Liu Zengfu 197, 206
  clerical script by 34, 35, 197
  The Evening of the Lantern Festival 197, 200, *200–1*

Ferrying South to Lizhou 197, *198–9*
Zhang Shizhao 75, 76, 77
Zhang Xu 20–1, 111, 168
Zhang Zhengyu 29, 119–24, 131, 166, 212
  Da Guan Lou Pavilion inscription by 122–3
  and Huang Miaozi 27, 174, 175
  scroll 27, *28–9*, 122–3
  Li Sao 121
  Ode to a Plum Blossom 122, *123*
  Premonition 120–1, 120–1
Zhao Mengfu 21, *21*, 67, 70, 77
Zhejiang Academy of Art, *see under* Hangzhou: China National Academy of Fine Arts

Zhenjiang, South Mountain Garden 207, 209
Zhou dynasty, bronzes 230
Zhou Enlai 204
  calligraphy by 45
  and Chen Yi 95, 96, 98
  death of 51–2, 89–90, 122, 124
  diplomatic relations with Japan 50, 142
  and Guo Moruo 51, 80, 81, 82, 87, 89–90
  and Huang Miaozi 173
  Jiang Qing's attacks on 128
  Lin Kai's poem 268, *269*
  met Sa Benjie 216
  poem from Qiao Guanhua 48–9
  and Sha Menghai 135
  and Shen Yinmo 71, 72, 73
  and Yang Xianyi 266, 267
Zhou Xingzi 201
Zhu Jiahua 133–4
Zhuangzi 102